Deliverance for Yourself and Others

A friend forever in Christ

Odette

By
Odette Ouellette

Cover design by Andrew Tubb

Published in Ottawa Ontario (Canada) by DocuLink
International.

National Library of Canada Cataloguing in Publication Data

Ouellette, Odette, 1943
 Deliverance for Yourself and Others

ISBN 0- 9684116-3-0

 1. **Spiritual warfare. 2. Demonology. 3. Spiritual life--**
Christianity. 4. Self-realization--Religious aspects--
Christianity.
I. Title.

BV4509.5.O93 2001   235'.4   C2001-903628-0

Dedication

I dedicate this book to the countless that came and were set free of Satan's bondage and also to share with others their victory.

To the numerous prayer warriors who interceded for me while writing this book. Your unceasing prayer gave me courage on a daily basis.

I express my heartfelt appreciation to my editors for their encouragement.

To Lynda Nelson and Diane Lee who graciously volunteered their talent and time in assisting in the correction of this book. Their outstanding contribution will help bring deliverance to the captives for generations to come.

To my niece, Lucie Brisson, for her secretarial expertise and computer skills in designing and putting my website on the Internet. You gave so much to spread the gospel and we praise God for the important part you played to bring the truth to those hurting around the world.

Most important of all my sincere gratitude to Our Father and Our Lord Jesus Christ for His guidance in writing this book. When new revelations are given, I stand in awe for I am a student under His leadership.

Introduction

After the publication of my first book on Discerning of Spirits the Unknown Gift the request I received the most from those who read the book was "Please give us more documentation on how to do deliverance on ourselves, our family, and in our church".

After many prayers, here is a layout on how spirits control our character and keep us in bondage. You don't have to stay a prisoner to these thieves.

This book is about how you can get started and learn what the prerequisites of deliverance are. You have the power in the name of Jesus Christ to break and renounce every spirit and mental torment in your life as a lie of the devil and be set free. So many people will deny that evil spirits are still in existence and controlling the lives of the body of Christ today. They keep saying deliverance was for two thousand years ago. They will use medical terms to cover the real name of the evil spirit. This is exactly what Satan wants. By denying that he is still oppressing the souls of God's people, Satan has an open door to keep churches, families and countries in bondage.

Christians have the power to release themselves and others from what the enemy is sending towards them. The gift of discerning of spirits was given to us believers and we can be set free in the precious Name of Our Lord Jesus Christ.

Contents

Chapter 1

Light Against Darkness

In the beginning when God formed all things, He first created the heavenly powers. *"For by him were all things created, that are in heaven, and that are in earth, visible and invisible, whether they be thrones, or dominions, or principalities, or powers: all things were created by him and for him. And he is before all things and by him all things consist." Col. 1:16-17 KJV*

When God created the heavens and the earth it was to last forever. This is seen in Ps. 104:5 and Eccl. 1:4. Also, Isa. 45:18 reveals, *"For thus saith the Lord that created the heavens; God himself that formed the earth and made it; he hath established it, he created it not in vain, he formed it to be inhabited: I am the Lord; and there is none else." KJV*

However, a war took place in the heavenlies when Lucifer, one of God's angels, became proud because of his beauty. Lucifer had ruled under the direction and authority of God. He had been perfect in all his ways but while he ruled, wickedness was found in him according to Ezek. 28:12-15. He became self-exalting, wanting to become like God and dethrone Him. He rebelled and led the invasion into the heavens as the scriptures tell us in Isa. 14:12-15; Ezek. 28:11-19; and Rev. 12:7-9. He was cast out of heaven, losing his dominion and taking all the other fallen angels with him. They are now confined to the heavenly surroundings of the earth, where he and his demons have set up their kingdom of havoc and destruction. This is where, in his subtle way, Satan is trying to regain the kingdom he has lost.

Satan has a government and there are levels of leadership in his kingdom. Eph. 6:12 describe this government as "principalities, powers, rulers of the darkness of this world and wicked spirits in the high places." Satan rules over his structure, dictating and controlling his demons. None have a will of their own. They are under his leadership and his direct command, destroying everything they touch.

This war happened before Adam's time. Satan was already a fallen angel when Adam was created and put in the Garden of Eden. We know this because he appeared to Adam and Eve in the Garden in the form of a serpent in Genesis Chapter 3.

Before this, however, in Genesis Chapters 1 & 2 we see the account of God creating the earth and everything in it and assigning to the male and female their roles and duties.

In Genesis 1:27-28 God created man and woman. The scriptures say, ***"So God created man in his own image, in the image of God created he him; male and female created he them. And God blessed them, and God said unto them, Be fruitful, and multiply, and replenish the earth, and subdue it: and have dominion over the fish of the sea, and over the fowl of the air, and over every living thing that moveth upon the earth." KJV***

In Genesis Chapter 2 we see the first marriage taking place. Adam & Eve became one flesh. We see in verse 25 that they were both naked and were not ashamed. They were sinless, gentle, soft, and very wise.

They were placed in this wonderful place to live and given authority over all of God's creation. However, there was one limitation placed on them. They could eat from any tree in the garden except one specific tree in the middle of the garden that God referred to as the tree of the knowledge of good and evil.

Now when God told Adam and Eve not to eat of the tree of the knowledge of good and evil, there was a reason for it. The fruit of the tree of the knowledge of good and evil, if eaten, would open their eyes to what was morally right and wrong. Any act of disobedience would create a separation between them and God causing them to die spiritually.

In Gen. 2:17 we read, *"But of the tree of the knowledge of good and evil, thou shalt not eat of it: for in the day that thou eatest thereof thou shalt surely die." KJV* God knew that if Adam and Eve disobeyed they would become slaves to the powers of darkness. Rom. 6:16 tells us: *"Do you not know that when you present yourselves to someone as slaves for obedience, you are slaves to the one whom you obey, either of sin resulting in death, or of obedience resulting in righteousness?" LB*

Here we see God doing two things: First, He gave man the responsibility of taking care of His creation and second, man was given a free will to choose to obey God or to go his own way.

Satan, who was watching, heard God's words and was furious because he knew that if Adam and Eve were to have dominion over every living thing then that also meant him. He thought to himself, "Not if I can help it."

His plan was to regain the authority and the world he had lost so he set out to cause the downfall of man.

Satan saw how Adam loved the beautiful wife that God had given him and how his heart melted when she captivated his attention. If Satan could make her fall then Adam would not be far behind because of his love for his mate.

He built a strategy to tempt Eve. By lying just a little bit and tempting her by appealing to the lust of the flesh or her pride, he could confuse her and make her doubt God. So, he appeared to her in the form of the serpent as we see in Gen. 3:1. ***"Really?" he asked. "None of the fruit of the garden? God says you mustn't eat any of it?" KJV.*** This question brought doubt for he misquoted God.

God had not said they could not eat from every tree of the garden. He said they could not eat from only one specific tree.

In his sneaky way, Satan aroused Eve's curiosity by twisting what God had said. Then, Satan asked her another question that brought more doubt. ***"God says you mustn't eat any of it?" LB***. We see in Gen. 3:4-6, ***"And the serpent said unto the woman, Ye shall not surely die: For God doth know that in the day ye eat thereof, then your eyes shall be opened, and ye shall be as gods, knowing good and evil. And when the woman saw that the tree was good for food, and that it was pleasant to the eyes, and a tree to be desired to make one wise, she took of the fruit thereof, and did eat, and gave also unto her husband with her; and he did eat."*** **KJV**

He lied, suggesting that the power she had was nothing compared to the power she could have if she ate the fruit. She would have God's power, God's authority and God's wisdom (Gen. 3:5). She desired to become self-sufficient and have the wisdom to make them as God.

What Satan failed to tell her was that although she would know the difference between good and evil, she would have a very hard time being good since she would be controlled by the lust of the flesh or the five senses.

Eve was deceived. She ignored God's command, rebelled and took of the fruit, ate it, and gave some to her husband who was with her. This is revealed in Gen. 3:6.

Adam didn't come to the defense of his wife or protect her. He didn't shelter or care for the kingdom that God had instructed him to protect, which included his wife. He voluntarily took of the fruit and ate with Eve.

Because of this disobedience and rebellion, Adam and Eve died spiritually the same day. Not a physical death but a spiritual one. They were both cursed to live a life apart from God. They unknowingly handed over to Satan the ability to manipulate their character.

When Adam and Eve disobeyed God and departed from the truth, Satan obtained a legal hold over them that brought bondage on all future generations. From being sinless they now became sinners. When their eyes were opened, it was a different story than what the enemy had told them it would be.

They may not have realized at that moment but because of their disobedience the whole human race would be forced to live in sin and misery.

In the evening God came to talk to Adam. Gen. 3:9-12 says: *"And the Lord called unto Adam, and said unto him, Where art thou? And he said, I heard thy voice in the garden, and I was afraid, because I was naked; and I hid myself. And he said, Who told thee that thou wast naked? Hast thou eaten of the tree, whereof I commanded thee that thou shoudest not eat? And the man said, The woman whom thou gavest to be with me, she gave me of the tree, and I did eat." KJV*

Here we see that when God asked Adam where he was Adam was filled with fear and could not even take responsibility for his own action.

First, he tried to put the blame on Eve for having given him the fruit and then he made sure to point out to God that He was partly to blame also for He was the one who had given him the woman in the first place. This was a weak excuse for his poor judgment.

Before eating the fruit, Adam and Eve were never afraid because they walked in close fellowship with God. But they broke that fellowship with God through their disobedience. Now their eyes were opened to good and evil and their conscience condemned them. Adam and Eve had lost their relationship with God and it was easy for spirits of fear, shame, guilt, cowardice and blame to enter them.

When Adam and Eve tried to become like God, it didn't go as planned. Instead they became powerless, corrupted, terrorized by fear and slaves to Satan's control. A curse came upon all the earth because of disobedience.

We are still paying the price of that curse to this day. Satan is still allowed to torment and oppress the children of God. This is the result of sin. And sin became stronger in the next generation. In the next paragraph we will see what the curse brought on the family.

In Gen. 4:1, Eve conceived and Cain was born. She conceived again and Abel was born. While growing up Cain became a farmer and his brother, Abel, was a shepherd. They would bring offerings to God.

Adam must have received some kind of information from God as to what kind of offering to present for mercy.

Cain came before God with a wrong heart as revealed in Gen. 4:5; 1 John 3:12, Heb. 11:4 and Jude 11. He knowingly presented the wrong offering by bringing the fruit of the land. In Prov. 21:27 we read, *"The sacrifice of the wicked is abomination: but how much more, when he bringeth with a wicked mind." KJV* Here you can see the self-will that was already in control of him. While growing up the spirits of disobedience, rebelliousness and unbelief came down to Cain through the genes or bloodline.

Abel, who was a more righteous man (as seen in 1 John 3:12) wanted to please God and he brought the right offering. Gen. 4:4 says, *"And Abel, he also brought of the firstlings of his flock and of the fat thereof. And the Lord had respect unto Abel and to his offering". KJV*

God accepted Abel's offering but not Cain's. The Bible is unclear as to how God accepted these offerings. Was the offering consumed by fire as seen in 1 Kings 18:36-37, Judges 6:17-21 or Lev. 9:24? We don't know.

However, if you look in Gen. 4:5 you will see that this made Cain angry, full of hate and dark with fury for his heart was not right with God. He was furious and a

spirit of murder dominated him. He killed his brother. Then, he openly lied to God in defiance and tried to hide his crime. We see this in verse 9, *"And the Lord said to Cain, Where is Abel your brother? And he said, I do not know. Am I my brother's keeper?" AMP*
What a legal hold Satan had over this young man's mind! Because there was no law yet for murder, God became the judge and the jury. And the penalties imposed on Cain for the criminal act he committed was to become a fugitive and vagabond for the rest of his life.

Can you imagine the hurt and pain Adam and Eve suffered when they realized they lost their two sons in one day; Abel to death and Cain to God's judgment of banishment? What ravage sin can cause in destroying a family.

By disobeying God, Adam and Eve lost their spiritual life, their communion with God, their perfect health, their power to do good and also their peaceful mind. They inherited instead God's judgment. The curse was put on the soil, upon all creation, they lost their perfect health and death came upon everyone and everything. They became rebellious and obstinate. They received eternal damnation. This was the result of the ravage of the fall.

Chapter 2

What is a Curse?

What is a curse? Webster's Dictionary defines it as: *"(1) an evil or injury that comes down to a person or thing, or (2) taking an oath or making a pact for injury on someone or oneself".*

If you go back to Genesis, God spoke the first curse recorded in the Bible. He put a curse on the serpent in Gen. 3:14. In verses 17-18, because of Adam's disobedience and turning away from God, a curse of painful toil came up on him and the ground and all its vegetation was cursed. This is an example of God speaking a curse.

In Deut. 28:1-14, you see the blessing that will be yours as a result of obedience. In verses 15-65, you see the curse that will come up on people because of disobedience or following their own self will. God can speak a curse or we can put one on ourselves and others. There are curses that are handed down from generation to generation. Scripture illustrates this in many instances.

I would like to bring to your attention how curses and the impact of curses came down through various Biblical family lines. You will see how the soil, the animals and substances such as poison, germs, disease, sickness and all other forms of adversity became man's penalty for disobedience. Here are just a few.

1. In Gen. 3:14, God spoke the first curse when He cursed the serpent to crawl and eat dust for the rest of his days.

2. In Gen. 3:16, a curse of pain and sorrow was put on Eve in bearing children because of her disobedience and rebellion. We are still under that curse as those who are bearing children, today, can testify.

3. In Gen. 3:17-19, a curse was put on the soil. The soil began to grow weeds better than food. Originally, when Adam gathered food it was easy but after the curse, it took hard labor for provisions. Curses causing difficulty and harsh work were placed on Adam and his descendents as punishment for his disobedience and rebellion.

4. In Gen. 4:8-9, 19 and 23, we see an example of generational curses through Cain (the first-born son of Adam) and later Cain's descendant Lamech. Cain's rebellion was a disrespectful attitude toward God and resulted in a violent temper. He became a murderer when he killed his brother. The curse followed in Cain's bloodline to five generations. Lamech had a violent temper. He became a murderer and a polygamist (Gen. 4:20). Do you think that the sin of Cain was forgotten? Not so! A door had been opened for the sins of the forefathers to be repeated in the next generation. It was transferred through his genes and the same curse got worse when reoccurring in his offspring. Corruption became so rampant in all of Adam's descendants that God brought judgment on the earth. Gen. 6:5 tells us, ***"And God saw that the wickedness of man was great in the earth and that every imagination of the thoughts of his heart was only evil continually." KJV***

5. Out of all this wickedness in Gen. 6:5, 11, Noah found grace and favor with God. It seemed that he was the only pure ancestry of Seth's descendants who had not intermarried with the pagan nation. God told Noah that He was going to destroy all living things on the earth because it had become too evil. And Noah, his family and a number of animals were saved from the flood. Gen. 9:20-21 tells us that after the flood, Noah planted himself a vineyard. He got himself in trouble with alcohol. He loved God but still had weaknesses in his flesh. He got drunk. As he lay uncovered in his tent, his youngest son, Ham saw his nakedness. What he did must have been terrible for it got Noah so furious that he didn't curse his own son but he cursed Ham's son. We see this in Gen. 9:24-25. It is hard to believe that a grandfather could curse his own grandchild. Even though Ham was the guilty one, the curse fell on his son, Canaan. The descendents of Ham became so morally degenerate that Nimrod in Gen. 10:8-10 and later Sodom and Gomorrah in Gen. 10:15-19 were the result of those spirits of perversion.

6. Gen. 19:30-37 tells us about Lot who lived in the cities of Sodom and Gomorrah, where homosexuality and incest were rampant. His daughters were raised in this breeding ground of filth. Guess what? His daughters conspired a deceitful plan. They betrayed their own father and got him drunk. While inebriated they lay with him and both got pregnant. Two sons were born out of these incestuous conceptions as seen in Gen.

19:37-38. Sex between family members is forbidden by God as revealed in Lev. 18:6-18. Lot's two daughters must have known that incest was forbidden. They were conceived in shame and both were cursed.

The Bible records this shameful history. These sons became the patriarchs of the Moabites and the Ammonites (Deut. 23:3-4; Judges 3:28-30; 2 Sam. 8:2; Neh. 12:1 and Zeph. 2:8-11). As you can see, their father died but their posterity paid a penalty for their diabolical plan. An example of transference of sin is revealed in Lam. 5:7 *"Our Fathers have sinned and are not and we have borne their iniquities." KJV*

7. In Gen. 16:3 we see that Abraham and Sarah went ahead of God's plan to have a child. They went ahead of God's plan because of a spirit of unbelief and impatience. These spirits controlled this family who, by their own self-will, tried to help God. Having been barren all her life, Sarah offered her maid, Hagar, to her husband so that she may conceive on Sarah's behalf. This was against God's law according to Gen. 2:24. We don't see any proof that Abraham objected to his wife's appeal for he complied with her request. He slept with the maid and she got pregnant, later delivering Ishmael. It brought trouble as seen in Gen. 4-6.

In time, Abraham and Sarah had their own son, Isaac. Sarah forced Abraham's oldest son, Ishmael, out of the tent. The birthright of the firstborn son was stolen according to the custom.

The curse of the stolen birthright jumped one generation but it followed the bloodline and showed up again in Isaacs' son, Jacob.

Abraham favored his youngest son, Isaac. Isaac favored his oldest son, Esau, while his wife, Rebekah favored the youngest son, Jacob. The same pattern of the sins of the fathers was repeated from generation to generation.

8. Jacob was forced to go away from home because of the conspiracy of Rebekah to steal the birthright from her firstborn son, Esau, and to give it to Jacob (Gen. 27:5-34). Later, Jacob's youngest son, Joseph was favored over the oldest, Reuben. Sin came down through the generations. A spirit of favoritism followed this family. This spirit of favoritism opened the door for the spirits of family strife, discord, jealousy and lying to come in. The curse of family breakup was still in action.

9. Abraham had two wives. A curse of polygamy came down through the bloodline. Two wives, Rachel and Leah, were forced on Jacob as seen in Gen. 29:18-30. The curse had not been forgotten. The curse jumped one generation and came down to Abraham's grandchild, Jacob. Spirits of jealousy, favoritism, envy, strife, division and wandering from the family were in control. These curses were repeated throughout consecutive generations. Jacob was deprived of his family and was rootless in another land. These curses were not broken.

10. In Gen. 37:23-36 Jacob's sons lied to their father because of hate, jealousy, envy and murder toward

their younger brother, Joseph. They told Jacob that Joseph was dead when, in fact, they had sold him into slavery. It caused Jacob extreme suffering. In Gen. 42:1-45 and 50:15-21, we see how they reaped what they sowed. Once again the curse was repeated down the bloodline. Joseph, like Jacob, was forced to leave home and was also deprived of his family and became rootless in another land.

11. We will move on to 1 Sam. 2:12-25 where we see Eli as a high priest in Israel. He was so busy guiding the people that he spoiled his sons rotten and they served the devil. They committed adultery, idolatry, robbed the people, and blasphemed God (1 Sam. 2:12-17). He didn't instruct or teach them in the ways of the Lord. Being of the Leviticus priesthood they weren't the example they should have been nor did they keep the law. Since they persisted in continuing in their sin, God had to destroy them. Eli was warned of this ahead of time through a prophecy given by the prophet Samuel. He was told that he would have no descendants (1 Sam. 2:27-33). His prophecy was fulfilled when both wicked sons were killed on the same day during a battle with the Philistines (1 Sam. 4:1-11). Eli himself was also destroyed when, upon hearing the news of his sons' deaths, fell backward off his chair and broke his neck (1 Sam. 4:18). Eli knew about the iniquity of his sons but he didn't do anything to stop them. They were living in sin and brought a curse upon themselves, which had to be broken.

12. In 1 Sam. 28:1-25 Saul, king of Israel, persisted to live in sin and the Spirit of God departed from him. Because of envy, self-will, covetousness and rebellion he lied to Samuel, the prophet, and was rejected as king. A demon spirit entered and controlled him. He was being tormented and controlled by the spirit of murder, jealousy and envy, daily. God didn't answer him anymore by dreams or by prophets. So when he needed answers he went to see a witch. A curse of death came on Saul because of his involvement with witchcraft. He was killed as well as his sons.

13. In 2 Sam. 5:3, David became king of Israel. A curse came on his household because of sin. He committed adultery with Bathsheba, the wife of Uriah (one of his soldiers). A child was conceived as a result of this adultery. To hide his sin he had Uriah killed in battle. As a result, a man of God prophesied that the sword would never depart from David's house (2 Samuel 12:10-12). David and his children were cursed by death, rebellion, rape, murder, strife, division, deception, war and disgrace. His son, Amnon, raped his half sister. His second son, Absalom, killed his half brother, Amnon for raping his sister. Absalom rebelled and tried to steal the throne from his father by turning Israel against him. War broke out and Absalom, the second son of David, was killed. In 1 Kings 2:24 Solomon had his half brother killed to suppress a revolt against his kingdom. And as you read through the scriptures, the sword never departed from David's lineage.

Sin was and is still today, rampant. The Bible gives many more examples of how curses were found and traveled throughout generations. I simply wanted to demonstrate how curses might have been formed in your own life through previous generations. Your ancestors paid a penalty for the transgression that came down to them because of Adam's disobedience. This transgression is still following your progeny to this day.

Curses can come upon people by a spoken word. Many times it is done out of anger and the person is not aware that a curse was spoken. I have seen a curse of death put on a wife by her husband through words spoken in anger.

Another had a curse of a dumb and stupid spirit placed on her by her parents. Verbal words of abuse and negativity were spoken to her all of her growing years. She gradually lost the will to try to see the truth and accepted these ravaging words as truth. She became dumb and stupid. A spirit had a crack to come in and destroy her life.

A young man was prone to having multiple car accidents. Only by the grace of God was his life spared. This curse came down to him by someone who wished him destruction. This is a curse of doom.

A young boy and girl innocently made a pact with Satan one day when playing. They had erected an altar and sacrificed an animal. They offered their soul to Satan. A curse came on them by their spoken words and actions. Their life was ravaged. A spirit of destruction followed them every step of their growing lives. Finally, out of desperation one of them committed suicide. This is an example of a self-uttered curse.

When a person consults a medium or a fortuneteller and lives by the zodiac and astrology signs to predict their future and to organize their daily lives, then a curse comes upon them. They are putting their trust in evil spiritual beings. They give permission to these thieves to control their every move.

Some innocently wear an astrological or occult sign around their necks to bring them good luck. A conjuration or a spell is then put on that person. They are asking another god for protection and to fulfill their requests.

I learned of another form of a spoken curse when a woman came for deliverance and the Holy Spirit revealed that someone had put a curse on her. When asked about it she explained, "My mother forced me to marry a man because he was wealthy. After a few years of marriage, I was very unhappy. I couldn't take it any more so I went to see my mom for advice. This is what she said to me, 'You made your bed, you lie in it'."

By forcing her to marry this man and stay in a marriage where there was no love or peace, a curse of unhappiness had been put on her by her mother.

Another way of cursing or applying a curse is when a person damns another person, object or thing like a car, electrical appliance, children, animals, etc. Many people do not have the remotest idea of the impact of their words. They will casually damn someone out of ignorance or they will do it intentionally out of revenge or anger. These are words that are endlessly repeated by friends, enemies, parents, husbands, wives, teachers and others. These words shape the mind and invite the enemy to weaken your defenses. And when you become discouraged, then he has a foothold to destroy your life. By entertaining and dwelling on negative thinking you involuntarily open a door to be harassed by the enemy.

Many curses are often self inflicted. By constantly repeating words of failure, you invite demonic spirits to deliver what you acknowledge. By saying, "my parents were poor and I will always be poor" you invite a curse of poverty. If you confess poverty all the time you will invite spirits of lack and destitution to destroy your finances and everything you work for.

If you confess all the time, "I can't remember a thing" a curse of lack of memory and forgetfulness will be your inheritance. You reap what you sow.

A woman said that every time she found work that she loved she lost her position. She kept saying, "Every time I love my workplace I am fired for no reason." She confessed these words of defeat and Satan made sure to have his lying spirits around to give her what she confessed daily.

"My parents divorced, my marriage will end in divorce also." This is a curse of family and marriage breakup. Negative confessions brought exactly what she acknowledged.

A man constantly said, "I am going to be sick. My family was sick all the time and so will I." The parents sowed sickness and infirmity and the son reaped the curse of bad health.

A wife often said to her husband "You will never amount to anything in life." As a result of her repeated condemnation, spirits of criticism, disapproval, denigration, and blaming others were invited into the household and the curse of failing was his fate.

A mother continually said to her son, "You are just like your father. You will be just as corrupt as he is. He was an alcoholic and a womanizer and you will turn out to be just like him. You watch and see." By constantly inviting these spirits into her home the curse of perversion was established and her son gradually believed what his mother kept telling him. He became exactly what she spoke on him.

Many parents don't give their young children a chance to learn how to train their clumsy little hands. Because of impatience, a parent may do everything for their youngster and if the child makes an attempt to try, they tell the young one "You are so awkward, you are such a klutz." By constantly repeating these discouraging admonitions, a door is opened and parents hand down a curse of being a klutz. Spoken words can become a curse.

If you have damned an adult, a child, an animal, an object, etc., break every curse that was spoken right now and revoke that curse in Jesus' name by saying the following prayer:

"Father in the name of Jesus Christ I believe you died on the cross for my sins and rose again from the dead. I believe you are the Son of God come in the flesh to destroy the works of the enemy. I now confess and repent of all my sins and I ask you to forgive me. I break all evil curse that was spoken over me and my family line. I renounce, break and loose every evil control, which have kept us in physical or mental bondage and illnesses as a result of our forefathers sin and curses. I renounce, break and loose every spirit

that torments, defiles or harasses me right now in Jesus name. I thank you Lord for setting me and my children free by the power of the Holy Spirit in Jesus name. Amen

According to the scriptures in James 3:9, 10, *"Therewith bless we God, even the Father; and therewith curse we men, which are made after the similitude of God. Out of the same mouth proceedeth blessing and cursing. My brethren, these things ought not so to be." KJV*

When you get away from the protection or covering of God and you follow your own self-will, then satan has the right to impose a pattern of destruction on you. However in Ps. 91 God promises to care for and rescue you from any trouble the enemy sends toward you if you stay under His wings. You can break any curse and any bondage in the name of Jesus. Gal. 3:13 says, *"Christ hath redeemed us from the curse of the law, being made a curse for us: for it is written, Cursed is every one that hangeth on a tree." KJV*

Jesus died a shameful death to redeem us from the curse of the law. By renouncing and breaking the curse of your forefathers, curses spoken over yourselves or curses spoken against you through others will free you from bondage. Your soul will be loosed from bondage and you will regain your authority over the power of darkness. You are not fighting against the sin of your neighbors but the sin of your family line. A curse might jump one generation but don't think your family will get away from it. The cycle or the penalty of disobedience will be handed down to the next descendants unless it is broken.

The Holy Spirit can reveal what kind of curse have been affecting and coming down to you. The curse can be discerned by the gift of discerning of spirits. You can reclaim your inheritance as in Deut. 28:1-14 by breaking the curses that came upon you and your offspring so that you may be blessed. Only the blood of the Lamb of God can reverse the curse.

Chapter 3

What Is Salvation?

Before you can receive spiritual deliverance you must be born again. In 1 Cor. 2:14 it says, *"But the natural man receiveth not the things of the Spirit of God: for they are foolishness unto him: neither can he know them because they are spiritually discerned." KJV*

Salvation is personal and no one can make that decision for you nor make the decision to stand as a substitute in your place. The only way to be cleansed from sin is through repentance and faith in the precious blood of our Lord Jesus Christ.

First, God loves us. The scriptures tell us in John 3:16, *"For God so loved the world, that he gave his only begotten Son, that whosoever believeth in him should not perish, but have everlasting life." KJV*

Second, sin separates us from God. Here is what the Scriptures say:

Romans 3:10 *"As it is written, There is none righteous, no, not one" KJV*

Romans 3:23 *"For all have sinned, and come short of the glory of God;" KJV*

Isaiah 59:2 *"But your iniquities have separated between you and your God, and your sins have hid his face from you, that he will not hear." KJV*

What we have inherited from Adam was not simply a stain that we can erase with a drop of water in a baptismal ceremony. The Bible does not state that the stain of the original sin can be removed by water. But because of one man's (Adam) disobedience, we all became sinners. Romans 5:12 tells us, *"Wherefore, as by one man sin entered into the world, and death by sin; and so death passed upon all men, for that all have sinned:" KJV*

Going to church every Sunday doesn't make you a child of God. While in a Bible class a person asked, "What does it mean to be born again?" The Bible class leader answered "Born again means going to church every Sunday." There are many people who have gone to church for years and have not been born again. Obviously that was not the right answer.

A young child from his physical birth has inherited a suitcase (sin) on his back, a baggage through generational sins as seen in Ex. 20:5 and 34:7. With no one teaching him how, he will start to disobey, get angry, tell lies and do many other things that will devastate his parents and have them wondering why. In Psalm 51:5 we read, *"Behold, I was shapen in iniquity; and in sin did my mother conceive me." KJV*

The only one who can redeem us from the curse of the law is Jesus Christ. John 3:5 says, *"Jesus answered, Verily, verily, I say unto thee, Except a man be born of water and of the Spirit, he cannot enter into the kingdom of God." KJV*

Even if you say that you have your religion and that you were baptized, confirmed and go to church every Sunday, this is still not the new birth. The liar, the adulterer, the one who blasphemes the name of God, the evil slanderer who takes pleasure in destroying the reputations of others, the drunkard and the thief, all have their religion. Neither their behavior nor their baptism has made them a child of God. Their actions and their conduct would definitely prove the opposite.

They think that if they go to church every Sunday, confess their sin, and, with no regrets, come out and start their immoral behavior all over again, their religions will save them. They assume they are going to make it to heaven. This is not what the Bible reveals.

Salvation is when you accept Jesus Christ as your personal Savior and you turn your back on sin. Salvation is when you renounce any worldly pleasure and every involvement with corrupt and wicked ways and not wanting to sin anymore. (In the dictionary, **"renounce"** means: to give up a habit, a practice or former things.) You focus your heart and mind on God and let Him be your judge.

The one who has not been redeemed from the curse of the law doesn't want to let go of their worldly chains and cannot be set free. To be forgiven of one's sin in the Old Testament, blood had to be shed over and over again. In the New Testament Jesus, who is the perfect Lamb of God, shed His Blood once and for all as explained in (Heb. 7:27). When we sin, we go directly to Him to be forgiven and delivered.

Jesus is a respecter of people. He will not push His way into your heart but will wait patiently for His children to let Him be the Lord of your lives. In other words, Jesus will become your deliverer and your gentle Master. He is filled with compassion and mercy and when you release your burdens to Him, He is willing to forgive and set you free from Satan's captivity.

Repentance is for the Christian who sincerely wants to walk closer with God. When a person comes for deliverance and sits on what I call the "hot seat," he/she must be willing to repent of bondages that the Holy Spirit reveals. An unwillingness to forgive will block the work of the Holy Spirit.

Being honest and sincere, with an eagerness to judge only themselves and not others, will free the Holy Spirit to do His work in their hearts. You can see this in Matt. 6:14-15, *"For if ye forgive men their trespasses, your heavenly Father will also forgive you: But if ye forgive not men their trespasses, neither will your Father forgive your trespasses." KJV*

According to 1 John 1:9, *"If we confess our sins, he is faithful and just to forgive us our sins, and to cleanses us from all unrighteousness.* KJV In Isa. 1:18, we learn that God promises to forgive us all our sins even if they are red as crimson and to cleanse us of all unrighteousness.

You might ask "Is God ready to forgive me all of my sins?" God who is so full of mercy is ready to forgive all who repents and forsake their wicked ways. All sin is an indication of selfishness and pride in some form.

When we come to the throne of mercy and are sincere in renouncing our selfish ways our wonderful Savior will forgive us our trespasses. If you want to accept Jesus Christ as your personal Lord and Savior pray the following prayer with all your heart.

The Sinner's Prayer

"Lord Jesus, forgive me all of my sins.
I believe you died on the cross for me.
I repent of my sins and I accept you
as my personal Lord and Savior.
I open the door of my heart and
invite you to come in.
Wash and cleanse me
of all unrighteousness.
I turn my back on sin and
I want to follow you
for the rest of my life.
In Jesus' Name.
Amen"

Chapter 4

How Curses Are Transmitted

When we sin we open the door for Satan, the deceiver, to influence us and get a hold on our lives. This influence or weakness is passed on to our children. They are born with a susceptibility to the same spirits we've allowed to control our actions.

One of the first battles that a new Christian has to overcome involves the pleasures of the flesh: what you see, hear, touch, taste, and smell - your five senses. You can't begin fighting in the spiritual realm if you haven't overcome the desires of the flesh. You have to depend completely on the Holy Spirit to guide and to reveal what is controlling you. To depend on anything else would mean depending on psychic powers or divination, which is witchcraft. (Witchcraft is when you use the power of the devil such as fortune telling. See chapter on psychic power).

The Holy Spirit may reveal, by the gift of discerning of spirits, a spirit of poverty. They may be susceptible to ancestral curses of poverty travelling down the family line. Financial emergencies often come right after they receive their paycheck: the car needs new brakes, the rent is increased, the washing machine breaks down, unforeseen expenses come up, etc. These evil spirits work in groups. The spirits of destitution, lack, want, privation, hand-to-mouth existence, difficulties and debt, often accompany the spirit of poverty.

A young woman had a very hard time finding work. She had not had her job very long before her manager started making sexual advances toward her. She refused his advances and automatically lost her employment. She kept asking herself, "What is wrong with me. I didn't do anything to attract this man's attention?" She had to depend on others for her financial means.

Later she found out that her father was a womanizer and had many adulterous affairs with numerous partners. She was suffering the results of his perversion by being the target of fornication by other men because, unknown to her, a spirit of lust was passed down to her.

A woman had a child out of wedlock and gave it up for adoption. It was later revealed that her daughter had a child out of wedlock that was also given up for adoption. The curse passed on to her daughter's daughter who also had a child out of wedlock. The spirit of a bastard child came down three generations and if it is not broken it will go down to the next generation.

A father had a business and made many crooked deals by lying and cheating his customers. His son couldn't keep his businesses and had a multitude of bankruptcies. What the father stole from others was now being stolen from his son. The descendants of this man are paying the price for his dishonesty.

A Christian man came to me wanting to know if deliverance could help him and his children. While growing up his children had experienced all kinds of weird manifestations that could not be explained: sudden apparitions would appear and scare them tremendously, doors would open suddenly for no apparent reason, the sound of knocking on the walls would be heard, pictures would fall to the floor, agonizing pain would be felt in their bodies that had doctors baffled and unable to find a clue to explain the symptoms, etc. These children went to bed at night and woke up in the middle of the night to find a presence standing by the side of their beds, scaring the daylights out of them.

I was having a deliverance session one night in this home. All of a sudden one of the young boys came up the stairs with his comforter over his head crying and saying someone was poking him while he was sleeping. He was paralyzed and terrorized by fear.

I asked the father if this happened often and he answered, "There is not one night that goes by that one or two of my children don't wake up crying or screaming in their sleep for no apparent reason."

Guess what? The great grandfather had opened a door for Satan to have a legal hold to control and harass his descendents. A curse was handed down because of his involvement with the occult and his grandchildren were paying the price.

A man had a business where he sold food to people. Without any apparent guilt, he sold corrupt victuals to his clients. Guess what? His son was even more corrupt than his father. No one could trust his word. He was a real con artist, deceiving people only until they got to know him and then he would lose everything he worked so hard to acquire. The father's sin was amplified when passed down to the son. Where the father enjoyed cheating others, the son paid the price for his own corruption. Lam. 5:7 says, ***"Our father's have sinned, and are not and we have borne their iniquities."*** **KJV**

I could go on and on but I want to show you that when you come under the judgment of the law there is a penalty for sin. Curses are handed down whether you want them or not. I hear parents say, "I would not hurt my children for the world." But they don't see any harm in getting involved in witchcraft, not realizing that their children are being damaged for a lifetime. They willingly bring a scavenger into their house to devour the minds of their precious offspring's. It is not a visible enemy but an invisible one lurking in every corner by their own participation in these occults practices.

A person can be set free of these curses by repenting and renouncing their involvement in these practices. They can ask God's forgiveness, and break every curse that was handed down through the bloodline. They will then have healing in their minds and their bodies will be restored to health. They will be able to claim back the inheritance that God had ordained for them from the beginning as seen in Col. 3:24, *"Knowing that of the Lord ye shall receive the reward of the inheritance: for ye serve the Lord Christ. KJV*

Chapter 5

Soul Ties

What are soul ties? Soul ties are formed when two or more person are bonded together through godly or ungodly relationship. When someone associates with evil followers it forms evil soul ties that brings rebellion, wickedness and perversion. It will entangled a person in sinfulness and will corrupt his moral and his character.

Good and pure soul ties are formed when bonding with friends through friendship (Pro. 17:17 and 18:24) and between Christians within a church in the bond of agape love as seen in Gal. 6:2.

Good soul ties are developed when it is based on love. Husbands and wives form holy and pure soul ties and are devoted and committed to one another.

In a marriage a soul tie is a connection or binding of an invisible knot between a husband and a wife. It is a spiritual bond instituted by God that forms as a result of physical intimacy and that holds a marriage together and it foster love and security.

The husband and wife are joined in one flesh and restrict their sexual desire to their partner only. Each has a moral accountability to the one they have promised to love and obey. They are bound by marriage. (Gen. 2:24)

When a good soul tie is formed, a bond of love will stabilize the relationship and it will not oppress or hinder the natural process of ministering love to others. It will not control or manipulate the character of another.

An evil soul tie is formed in different ways and generally falls into three categories.

One category is when natural boundaries have been violated by joining oneself to another person through fornication, adultery, incest, homosexuality or lesbianism. This is the unnatural sexual relations category.

The second category deals with mind control domination by parents, children, in-laws, companions, etc.

Thirdly, evil soul ties are formed when trying to acquire knowledge or power through demonic sources such as fortunetellers, tarot cards, astrology, etc. This opens the door for an evil occult soul tie to occur. The demonic control will ensnare a person and manipulate their morals, their minds and their character. It's like an invisible rope attaching them to the other person and they cannot get rid of it. It binds a person in their thoughts and bodies and no matter how much they want to liberate themselves, the mental torment is always there. Only through deliverance can these soul ties be broken and a person be set free.

I would like to expand upon these three categories to illustrate the workings of soul ties.

Unnatural Sexual Relations

An evil soul tie is formed when a spirit of lust transfers its character to the person. A person with a spirit of lust acts with seductive charms and their language and clothing will be very explicit. They walk with a sexual body language to entice by flirtations. Their whole personality will be affected.

In a marriage, if one breaks their marriage vows by committing adultery or having even one sexual encounter outside of marriage, a door is opened for unclean spirits to transfer to their spouse and they are defiled.

God tells us in Scripture that by joining one another through sexual intercourse, soul ties are formed and the two become one in God's sight. 1 Cor. 6:16 says, *"And don't you know that if a man joins himself to a prostitute she becomes a part of him and he becomes a part of her? For God tells us in the Scripture that in his sight the two become one person." LB* (Verify also in Matt. 19:5)

Sexual relationships outside of marriage will cause a demonic stronghold. The man and woman involved in this encounter are not married on paper but they are in body and soul as a result of the sexual union.

When an evil soul tie is formed through adultery it destroys the oneness in the married couple. When the other partner has been betrayed it is hard to restore the oneness and trust that was there before. No matter how much the guilty party regrets his/her actions there will always be suspicion or distrust. This develops into jealousy that often ends in divorce.

When a divorce takes place because of broken vows it's like ripping the heart of those involved. The hurt, the pain, the sorrow caused by the divorce is indescribable. The one who has gone through it will even go as far as to say that it is worse than death. That's how tragic divorce will traumatized the individual.

Even after a divorce, soul ties between a husband and a wife are still invisibly attached. Although they are divorced on paper, the soul tie has not been broken. Because of the oneness of the flesh, they always seem to be connected to one another no matter how long ago the divorce has taken place. When a divorce takes place you are still attached by a soul tie to the first husband or wife. It's like an invisible bond that connects you to the other partner and unless you cut it, you will be hindered by recurring thoughts.

You will have to break every soul tie to your first wife/husband that was formed through marriage. God hates divorce but when one takes place because of fornication then if you want to be set free of mental torment you will have to break every bond that is still holding you captive.

How far can it go? When the spirit of adultery or fornication enters a person's soul or if it is already there by the sin of the forefathers, the individual loses control. These spirits of impurity, fantasy, adultery, oral sex, voyeurism and perversion are ruling him/her. A spirit of whoredom is controlling their every move. Their appetite for sex is insatiable.

Just when they think they have reached the most wonderful experience, they find they need more. They become more deeply involved and they never have enough of the filth.

Another way a soul tie is created is through perverted acts like incest, homosexuality, evil companions, family, ex-boyfriends/girlfriends, sexual acquaintances, etc. In 2 Samuel 13:1-20 we see an example of an obsessive controlling behavior in the story of Amnon and Tamar. He had lusted and longed for his half-sister for so long that he was obsessed with a spirit of lust. He was living daily in sensual and unlawful passions for his half-sister. He lied to his father, David, pretending he was sick so his father would send for Tamar to bake cakes for him to help his illness. It was his way of conniving to get Tamar into his house to force himself on her and rape her.

When his father, David found out about it he closed his eyes to what happened. No punishment followed. A wall of silence was kept over the matter. David became a cooperator and an accomplice to his son's brutal act.

The same thing is happening today. Children are forced to perform sexual acts that adults are obsessed with. Because pornography is so rampant individuals are acting like Amnon forcing and raping young children and teenagers like brute beasts and are getting away with it because of a wall of silence.

If an uncle, brother, father, friend, pastor, priest or acquaintance, etc. molests a child, they are often responsible for many of these innocent victims becoming homosexuals or lesbians. Unknown to the injured party, links are still attaching them to these people. They are bound by recurring pornographic thoughts and lust. They cannot be set free of the guilt and shame unless they break the soul tie that still connects them to the perpetrator

The spirits of perversion, fornication and lust are so integrated in our society that they've become regular members in family households. The counterfeit is infiltrating our homes. Your children openly watch lustful scenes on television, hear perverted language in schoolyards, read vile words in magazines, and taste the sexual violence in theatres. Sexually lewd entertainers have become their role models. And a child, not knowing the difference between what is real and what is unreal, commits in real life, the crimes they've seen acted in movies. They've become desensitized and demoralized, thinking that love is sex and that they can mess around without getting scarred.

Parents who are promoting these lifestyles of immorality and violence often write these scripts. Make no mistake. Children are like sponges. They absorb and assimilate bad habits from their parents. I would like to share an example of how a bad behavior was conveyed to a child.

One young woman saw nothing wrong in leaving the door open while she was having sexual intercourse with her boyfriend. Her daughter, passing in front of her mother's bedroom, would witness their sexual acts.

I explained to her how Satan was exposing her daughter to the spirits of lust, masturbation, fornication, provocation and sexual promiscuity. I shared these verses in Rom. 1:21-22; *"Because that, when they knew God, they glorified him not as God, neither were thankful; but became vain in their imaginations, and their foolish heart was darkened. Professing themselves to be wise, they became fools." KJV*

After hearing this, she was devastated. She explained that she had taken some courses promoted by the new age movement, and they had told her not to be ashamed of her body and to do whatever she pleased. She trusted them explicitly. By indulging in whatever she felt like doing she destroyed a marriage to a wonderful husband. With no concern for those around her, she partook of illicit affairs and lived her life with foolish abandon. Ungodly soul ties of perversion ensnared and entangled her in the filth of corruption.

Unknown to her, Satan was preparing a breeding ground for her young daughter for his service. Not having a role model in her home to pattern her life after while she was growing up, this child is now reaping the results of her mother's corrupt and permissive ways.

She grew into an uncontrollable teenager and is today living an immoral lifestyle, bound by the same spirits as her mother, and under the control of drugs and alcohol.

The mother, who is now a Christian and has been set free from the spirit of perversion, now has her spiritual eyes open to her daughter's bondage. She is crying bitter tears and has sleepless nights wondering where her daughter is and fearing for her safety.

If you choose to follow an immoral life style don't be surprised to see your children walking in your footsteps. Rather, teach your children the outcome of sin. Don't wait until they are in their teens to enlighten them.

It is the duty of every parent to instill within the hearts of their child the wisdom and knowledge of God. The purpose of hearing the Word of the Bible is to learn obedience and to trust in our Lord's protection against all enemies.

When God gave His laws to Moses He told him to teach the children also. In Deut. 4:9 it says, *"But watch out! Be very careful never to forget what you have seen*

God doing for you. May his miracles have a deep and permanent effect upon your lives! Tell your children and your grandchildren about the glorious miracles he did." LB

I will give you another example of how a curse was brought down to someone's offspring because of self-will. A Christian woman came to my home for deliverance. She confided in me that she was having an extra-marital affair and wondered if she could have deliverance and still continue having her extra-marital affair.

I answered, "No, you can't. How can you live a righteous life for Christ if you have adultery in your life? If you desire to be set free you must be willing to let go of the sin that has set up dominion in your life, having a firm commitment and desire never to practice it again."

She wanted to be set free of the mental torment and the guilt she was experiencing daily but at the same time she wanted to keep her adulterous relationship. The spirits of lust, perversion, hypocrisy, lasciviousness and adultery were in control. She desired to serve God, but the lust of the flesh was her Master. She refused to let go of her lover and the session was ended. She really thought that she could keep this adultery hidden from her husband and children. But unbeknownst to her the curse of adultery was handed down to her children and the future generations would pay the price for her secret pleasures.

In our country the spirits of illegitimacy are rampant. Today people don't think twice of living common law or having children before marriage. Because of ignorance of the scripture, they don't realize the truth of Deut. 23:2, *"A bastard shall not enter into the congregation of the Lord; even to his tenth generation shall he not enter into the congregation of the Lord." KJV*

If they don't give their lives to God and break the curse over themselves and their children, their descendants will reap the consequences of their actions for ten generations that equals about 400 years. Eph. 5:11,12,13 tells us, *"And have no fellowship with the unfruitful works of darkness, but rather reprove them. For it is a shame even to speak of those things which are done of them in secret. But all things that are reproved are made manifest by the light: for whatsoever doth made manifested is light." KJV*

Many times an unwanted pregnancy will cause the child to feel rejected within the womb and they will never feel loved or wanted. Jesus, by dying on the cross, provided the means to be delivered from this curse in His Precious Name as seen in 1John 5:13-15.

Mind Control and Domination By Parents

Soul ties can happen when there is an obsessive controlling or manipulation by teachers, religious leaders, doctors, psychics, children, the ungodly, etc. Recently we've seen examples of this especially in regard to religion. Jonestown is a good example of obsessive controlling by a cult but often some mainstream religious show manipulation and controlling of their supporters. The leadership wants the church congregation to be at their fingertips when they give a command. They also want their members to be at every service and every church function (and there are many). The church members are so concentrated on all these duties that they don't have time to be still and know that God is there. They even neglect their own family for fear of offending the controlling one. They concentrate all their attention on the pastor and they forget to ask God for their answers. They idolize the pastor and he becomes their god. If they disagree on the doctrine they teach they become an outcast. Ungodly soul ties need to be broken because of this mind control.

Another way soul ties are formed is by abnormal control by parents. When a child is born it is normal to have soul ties to the parents. A bond develops between mother, father and child promoting love and a cherished feeling. The infant, in his growing years, will feel secure and will become stable in his character and personality.

As the child grows up, the duty of the parent is to teach them how to make good choices and take responsibility. If they make wrong decisions then they will learn by their trials and errors.

However, if youngsters are raised being dependant on the approval or advice of others for making decisions, then the future consequences will be damaging. It becomes out of hand when parents try to manipulate or control their child's mind. In other words they do not cut the apron strings or soul tie. They are not letting their adult child think for himself, live his own life, make mistakes and sometimes fail as they did.

The parents forget that they gained wisdom through their mistakes; they want to save their children the trials of life. As a result, some children never grow up. They are always running to papa and mama to tell them what to do. This is a very unhealthy soul tie that many times will destroy the young person's life.

Prolonged Mourning

Another soul tie is formed when prolonged mourning takes place after the death of a loved one. Because people don't stop clinging to the memories, their grief is extended and a spirit of grieving, crying, sobbing and mourning enters and the sorrowful process is longer than required.

In the Bible, there were a certain number of days which were set apart after the loss of a loved one. In Deut. 34:8, grieving for Moses was 30 days. In Gen. 50:10, grieving for Jacob was 7 days. In Num. 20:29, grieving for Aaron was 30 days. In John 11:17, grieving for Lazarus was 4 days. In Mt. 12:40, grieving for Christ was 3 days. But after the funeral was over, they didn't grieve indefinitely. The days for mourning and grieving were limited. Indefinite grief is not a healthy situation for everyone.

There is a process of grieving after the death of a loved one. However, I have seen people who, having lost their father ten years ago, are still mourning. Mourning became an obsession, and there was an ungodly soul tie that was never severed. They had never been set free from the mental torment over the loss of their precious one.

Some adult children who have never severed emotionally from their parents and who have never learned to make decisions without their approval will be the most devastated by the loss of their precious ones. This is why the mourning process is extended beyond normal time. Because they could not function in any venture without being told what to do, they are now lost. Adjustments have to be made. They need to take control and responsibility for their own lives and learn to make decisions for themselves. They must start to grow up. To do that, the first step is to break every soul tie to the dead relative who was doing all their thinking for them and release them. Releasing means to give up to God the claim on the decease one to see them again at the resurrection according to 1 Cor. 15:22, 53, 55.

I remember visiting one family whose young child had been dead for four years, yet the living room was still filled with the child's toys and paraphernalia. They were still mourning after all these years. They were not releasing the child and if a word was mentioned about the little one, tears were still shed. There was an ungodly soul tie attached to that loved one. It was easy to believe in death, but they were not able to believe in the resurrection. They had no faith in our Lord Jesus Christ who gave His life that whosoever believed in Him would have everlasting life. John 3:16.

Seeking Knowledge Through the Occult

Soul ties can occur when one wants to find out about their future by use of witchcraft. There are many reasons why people go to mediums. For some, it is trying a new experience that they think will be just for fun. Others, wanting to spare themselves the unending pain of searching for a husband or wife, or wanting to invest in a business without risk, or even wanting to know what tomorrow has in store for them. They start their search by consulting a witch or medium. Some even go to sorcerers or dabble in sorcery themselves as a result of being disillusioned by their religions. Still others, wanting to be accepted, or seeking personal power, get involved with witchcraft. Then there are those who, while maintaining a sinful lifestyle and are unwilling to change, embrace witchcraft as a means of gaining approval. Their conscience is eating at them daily because of sin and guilt and they get involved in witchcraft to find new meaning to their life.

The unsuspecting one will innocently believe every word these people convey, never realizing how good a liar the devil can be. They do not realize that the minute they go to the spiritist for their answers an unholy soul tie is formed linking them to these people who will seek to control their minds through evil spirits. Physical and mental oppression will be the result, often with the person wondering what is oppressing them. Gradually as they get more involved, they become more confused and fearful, suffer from great guilt, and become more reclusive as they always fear impending doom.

By their participation in these activities a door is opened for evil spirits to harass and torment them daily with paralyzing fear, suspicion and dread. By seeking out these people, consent was unknowingly given and they are ensnared by the psychic power. They want out but don't know how to be set free.

James 4:7-8 tells us that we can be set free from the works of darkness by being delivered of the enemies bondage. Many Christians believe the enemy has no legal rights over them. They are therefore careless and give him authority unknowingly.

Once we repent before the Lord then and only then do we take away his privileges. That way the Christian will develop a vigilant lifestyle, being careful not to give the enemy any legal rights over them.

Do you want to break unhealthy soul ties? You say this prayer and tell Satan he has no control over you. You can break every unholy soul ties that has affected your life by praying the following prayer:

"Lord, in the name of Jesus, I ask forgiveness for every unholy soul tie that was formed by my ancestors or me; those known and those committed out of ignorance. I cut, break, bind and revoke every one of these unholy soul ties that still bind me to: (parents, husband, wife, children, teacher, pastor, church, religion, ex-boyfriend, girlfriend, buddies, adulterers, cults, occult, fortune telling, witches, animals, bloodcovenants formed outside of marriage or, mind control and manipulation. I break, renounce and revoke every one of these curses in the name of Jesus. I ask forgiveness for my involvement in these sins and I Thank you, Lord, for setting me free."

Chapter 6

Familiar Spirits

One thing Satan wants most of all is to be worshiped and glorified. He is jealous and envious of the adoration given to God and he will try, by every means, to steal it away from our Savior. The first commandment in Exodus 20:3 says, ***"Thou shalt have no other gods before me."*** **KJV**

The scriptures warn us that in the last days occult practices will be rampant. Multitudes of people, Christian and non-Christian alike, are being enticed by the occult. Satan, the deceiver, is luring multitudes of unsuspecting people by different approaches. 1 Tim. 4:1 explains, ***"Now the Spirit speaketh expressly, that in the latter times some shall depart from the faith, giving heed to seducing spirits, and doctrines of devils."*** **KJV**

These seducing spirits and doctrines of the devils are what we refer to when speaking of familiar spirits. The Bible has given us a guideline to follow that prohibits us from getting involved with these spirits. Here are 12 practices that describe familiar spirits and the scriptures where they can be found.

1. Enchantment - A practice of magical arts or of casting a spell. References in the Bible are in Ex. 7:11, 8:7; 8:18; Lev. 19:26; Deut. 18:10; 2 Chr. 33:6; Isa. 47: 9; and Jer. 27: 9.
2. Witchcraft - Supernatural power acquired by contacting evil spirits. Deut. 18:10; 1 Sam. 15:23; 2 Chr. 33:6; 2 King 9:22; Micah 5:12; and Gal. 5:19-21.

3. Sorcery - A supposed or imposed supernatural power over people and their affairs. This is the same as witchcraft. Ex. 7:11; Isa. 47:9-12, 57:3; Jer. 27:9; Dan. 2:2; Mal. 3:5; Acts 8:9-11, Acts 13:8; and Rev. 9:21, 18:23, 21:8, 22:15.

4. Sooth-saying - Foretelling the future. Once again this is similar to witchcraft. Isa. 2:6, Dan. 2:27, 4:7, 5:7, 5:11; Acts 16:16; and Micah 5:12.

5. Divination - The practice of trying to foretell the future or gain information about people or events by supernatural means. Deut. 18:10; 2 Kings 17:17; Jer. 27: 9-10; Jer. 29: 8; Ezek. 13:6-7; and Acts 16:16.

6. Magic - Any inexplicable power or influence produced by charms, spells, rituals and illusions by ruse or trick of the hand. Dan. 2:27-28; Gen. 41:8; Ex. 8:18-19; Ex. 9:11; Ezek 13:20.

7. Wizardry - A wizard (male) and a witch (female) are those who practice witchcraft, conjure or summon demon spirits to appear by use of magic. 2 Chr. 33:6; Lev. 19:31; Lev. 20:6, 27; Deut. 18:9-12; 2 Kings 23:24; and 2 Chr. 33:6.

8. Necromancy - Divination by alleged communication with the dead. One who prays to the dead or asks favors from them is practicing necromancy. Deut. 18:11; Isaiah 19:3; and 1 Chr. 10:13-14.

9. Charm - A powerful influence by a person who seduces another by exercising charm. Enchantment is another word for it. Isaiah 8:19-20; and Deut. 18:11.

10. Prognostication - To predict or foretell events by omens, astrology, horoscopes and stars. Isa. 19:26; Deut. 18:10; 2 Kings 21:6; and 2 Chr. 33:6.
11. Observing times - An act or practice of observing events by divination, imagining omens in the skies, and being superstitious of good days or unlucky days. Lev. 19:26; Deut. 18:10; 2 Kings 21:6; and 2 Chr. 33:6.
12. Astrology and Stargazing - To foretell the future by studying the influence of the moon, sun and stars of human affairs. It is a form of divination. Isa. 47:12-13; Dan. 1:19-20; and Dan. 2:1-28.

Familiar Spirit Involvement

Many things draw people into the realm of familiar spirits. For some it is curiosity, a fascination for or wanting increased knowledge of the supernatural realm. Some people, looking for guidance in their spiritual journey, have become disillusioned and lost faith in the religious system. Others, loaded with guilt are looking for ways to deal with their problems so they start looking for some other spiritual replacement to meet their needs. All of these become easy prey for Satan to lure and deceive.

There are people who are ensnared by those who claim they can reveal the unknown by fortune telling or relieve others of some kind of suffering by use of magical powers. Young people are being enticed into these groups through games such as Dungeons and Dragons, movies and books on the occult and drugs. Drugs alter a person's state of awareness and can cause people to do things that they would never think of doing when not drugged.

Many are deceived when they start to communicate with departed souls by necromancy. (Necromancy is when a person contacts or prays to a deceased person asking advice on how to proceed with their life, not realizing that they are asking an evil spirit to enlighten them.) They are enticed into these deceiving practices thinking that they are getting the knowledge from God. As you can see in Luke 16:19-31, Jesus was using this parable to show that dead people could not grant any requests. The only one who has the key (which signifies power and authority) to hell and death is Jesus Christ as is revealed in Rev. 1:18.

I have seen mothers quite innocently encourage their children to communicate with their dead fathers. Their religion had wrongly taught them to pray for the departed souls, thus, deceiving them and their children. Most of them only wish to help ease the pain of their loved ones. They do not intend to harm anyone but because of a lack of knowledge they are mislead into contacting these familiar spirits. In Hosea 4:6 we learn, *"My people are destroyed for lack of knowledge..."*

Some are recruited into the New Age Movement as a result of a fascination with the unknown. Many people go to New Age gatherings and swallow an entire teaching without even questioning whether or not it's true. The high-ranking of these esoteric or occult philosophies manipulate their victims by promising they will have supernatural powers.

Satan deludes many leaders in believing that God is really speaking to them, while others know that Satan is their master. They control their victims with lies. They have a way of appealing to the weak nature of searchers by listening intently to make them feel special and important, drawing in their victims. The victim then becomes a breeding ground for evil spirits to control their every move.

These leaders tell the innocent ones that they will have great power, be very rich, in control and have divine revelations. They mix some truths of the Bible with their false teaching and because of ignorance of the scriptures, the apprentice is easily deceived. The leaders will entice them by promising them that they will experience joy, along with a feeling of power, as they are led by their spirit guides. By pretending to have divine revelation themselves they encourage their victims to improve themselves, find their true identity and get in contact with their own spirit guide.

The superstitious one keeps looking for signs, wonders and guidance through a large diversity of expensive courses that are promoted in the occult movement. Some of these are new names but it is the same deceiving spirit behind all these magical arts. Here are some of these courses:

Remote Influence of the Subconscious Mind of Others
Therapeutic Touch for Health
Ecoute ton corps (which means listen to your body)
Altered State of Consciousness
Magnetic Alignment of the Chakra
Spirit of Metaphysical Healing
Fortune Telling   How to Develop Mind Control
Astrology   Trances for Diagnostic Treatment

Divination	Astral Projection
Magic	"Water Witching" or Dowsing
Magical Arts	How to Use your ESP
Spiritism	Age of Aquarius
Hypnosis	Transcendental Meditation
Sound Therapy	Crystal Reflexology
Palmistry	Regression Levitation
Numerology	How to Play Games
Innerquest	Silva Mind Control
Black Magic	False Religious Cults
White Magic	Casting Spells
Reiki	Shamanism
Voodoo	Tarot Cards
Acupuncture	Visualization
Acupressure	Clairvoyance
Sorcery	Magnetic Healing
Occultism	Reincarnation
Chakras	Games and Toys
Yoga	Kinesiology
Charming	Horoscope
Table-tipping	Turaya Touch
False Dreams	Harry Potter

After getting involved in the New Age Movement, one person shared some of the things that were happening in her life. She found herself afraid to make decisions, becoming increasingly confused and very suspicious. She was always asking her spirit guide for guidance. She was like a robot with no will of her own.

Her children awakened her one night crying in fear and saying that there was a black presence in their room. She became dissatisfied with her husband and her uncontrollable children and wanted to leave them. By bringing this oppression in the house, the whole family was under bondage. It brought strife and division in her marriage.

Consequences of Occult Participation

For some who participate in these practices, bad luck seems to follow them. For example, some have told of car crashes, losing money, developing sickness, being terrorized by fears, having nervous breakdowns, etc. After their involvement, many say that they want to commit suicide.

These things have been revealed or disclosed by those who have come out of these bondages. The scripture reveals that for those who get involved in the occult (Rev. 21:8) and transgress against God, the following will be the penalty for their sin if they don't repent. *"But the fearful, and unbelieving, and the abominable, and murderers, and the whoremongers, and sorcerers, and idolaters, and all liars, shall have their part in the lake which burneth with fire and brimstone: which is the second death." KJV*

The teachers do not tell their followers that this will be the result of their involvement in the occult. Any form of involvement in these practices is dangerous and can cause people to become ensnared.

Today, countless are searching for truth but do not know how to differentiate between the power of God and the power of Satan. In 2 Tim. 3:13 the scriptures explain, *"In fact evil men and false teachers will become worse and worse deceiving many, they themselves having been deceived by Satan"* and in *Matt. 24:24: "And there shall arise false Christ and false prophets and shall shew great signs and wonders; insomuch that if it were possible they shall deceive the very elect." LB*

Are You Oppressed?

Many are asking what signs they can look for which show that evil spirits are oppressing them or whether there is a curse on their family. How do you know if you are oppressed by the powers of darkness? I will try to show some of the symptoms that might be present in your life which point to demonic oppression and will affect your behavior.

1. If you have uncontrollable thoughts that keep coming into your mind of a sexual nature. If you have been involved in pornography, prostitution, masturbation, rape, sexual abuse, homosexuality.... you have unclean spirits operating in your life. You have an open door to your mind where evil spirits of perversion can control your thoughts.
2. If you are controlled by addictions to drugs, alcohol, food, gambling, nicotine, and you cannot stop yourself even when you try, any one of these could indicate infiltration of the enemy.
3. If you fly off the handle or throw temper tantrums for no apparent reason and get violent, feeling uncontrollable rage, murder, cruelty, destruction, hate, etc. then look for thieves in your house (body).

4. Do you have an obsession to commit suicide, mutilate or torture yourself? Satan's goal is to destroy you before your time.
5. If you are being controlled and manipulated by a cult, or obsessed with occult practices such as astrology, horoscopes, fortune-telling, psychic healing, handwriting analysis, Masons, Ouija board, ESP, books or movies on the occult or witchcraft, hypnosis, occult jewelry, heavy metal music, sorcery and drugs, then these are deceiving spirits in action and Satan is the perpetrator behind these bondages.
6. If you are prone to feelings or thoughts of jealousy, pain, shame, grief, sorrow, fear, greed, stealing, poverty, worry, confusion, pride, weak mindedness, unforgiveness, criticism, self-pity, discouragement, laziness, competitiveness, possessiveness, loneliness, rejection, phobias of all kinds then demons could be at work. But note: If a spirit is in control of your personality and you are out of control, you are incapable of stopping the enemy in your own power. Only in the power of Jesus Christ can the bondage be broken.
7. Tragic accidents, disastrous or heartbreaking events taking place in your family can be a result or indication of demonic forces at work to bring destruction.
8. Another tactic of the enemy is to infiltrate a home and to control a family with spirits of marriage and family breakup that bring curses of divorce.
9. There are some that are demonically tormented and controlled in their mind causing mental disorders such as restlessness, insomnia, inner anguish, emotional

breakdown, schizophrenia.... (Note: Not all mental disorders are caused by demonic oppression. Another source, which can cause mental disorders is a chemical imbalance caused by allergies, hormonal defects or poor diet.)

Here is an example of a lady who was unaware of the tactics of the enemy to bring destruction on her. She was innocently encouraged by her friend to study Reiki. She was unaware of the deception until she got to her third level. That night during a Reiki session she ended the teaching she had received with the phrase, "In Jesus Name." The leader of the group said angrily: "We don't want this name to be mentioned again in our meeting as it takes all our power away from us."

She then realized Reiki was not of God and quit the group. Because of a lack of knowledge she never suspected that this was a technique, which was probably thousands of years old and was greatly used by Tibetan Buddhists. The words "Rei" and "ki" are from the Japanese language. Rei means universal and ki is the life force energy that flows through all living things.

Shaman uses the same energy for spiritual development as well as for healing. Supposedly, there are seven main Chakra. They are located at the beginning of the crown of the head and continue to the Third Eye (between the two eyes), throat, heart, solar plexus, sex organs and the base of the spine or tailbone. These Chakras feed the body's organs with life force or chi. These points match the areas pierced by needles in the practice of acupuncture.

When learning to tap into this soul energy they unknowingly develop an occult power that opens a door for Satan to control them. This power to heal doesn't come from God. The only way to be healed or redeemed from the curse of slavery to sin and sickness is the shed blood of Jesus Christ as the scriptures tell us in Gal. 3:13. Any other way is done by Satanic power and brings destruction as revealed in Jn. 10:10.

Idol Worship

The practices of consulting familiar spirits were a custom greatly propagated by the heathen people in the Old Testament. The scriptures clearly specify that those who get involved with these familiar spirits have a curse on them according to Lev. 19:31, 20:6, 20:27; Deut. 18:11; 1 Sam. 28:3, 7, 8, 9; 2 Kings 21:6, 23:24; I Chr. 10:13; 2 Chr. 33:6; and Isa. 8:19, 19:3, 29:4. Some didn't believe in the one and only true God and made idols for themselves.

To be able to worship, religious people had a representation of a divine presence or statue in various places. The walls in some homes were covered with these images. The same thing is happening today. People today are worshipping other gods openly and seeking out familiar spirits more and more frequently.

In 1 Tim. 4:1 the apostles explained; *"Now the Spirit speaketh expressly, that in the latter times some shall depart from the faith, giving heed to seducing spirits, and doctrines of devils." KJV*

Many of the ancient nations would shed human blood before their gods. Those who practice voodoo do the same thing today. Their god is the counterfeit. They promote rites for the dead. This same thing is happening in our country.

Today, when a family member dies relatives go to funeral homes, touch the dead corpse, kiss it, pray over it and ask favors of it. Others make patron saints of people who have died and worship them. Numerous people start to pray to them, committing idolatry.

In the past, images were venerated and kissed. People prayed in the name of the martyred and, unknown to them, practiced necromancy. Still others made pilgrimages to worship relics wanting to receive revelations or healings from them. These relics became idols.

We see the same thing happening today. Today, as in the past, beings appear. If you have visitations from any dead beings and they ask to be worshiped – beware! These representations of saints are not from God. In 2 Cor. 11:14 we see, *"Yet I am not surprised! Satan can change himself into an angel of light." TLB*

The ancients would consult, pray to and ask favors of statues made of brass or silver representing their gods as seen here in Jer. 7:17-18, *"Do you not see what they are doing in the cities of Judah and in the streets of Jerusalem? The children gather wood, the fathers kindle the fire, and the women knead the dough, to make cakes for the queen of heaven; and they pour out drink offerings to other gods, that they may provoke Me to anger!"* **AB**

Being ignorant of the Law of Moses the people of Judah in the land of Egypt had backslidden so much that they worshipped the queen of heaven, the moon goddess, (whose name was Astarte, the wife of Baal or Molech). Because of idolatry and worshipping other gods, a curse of disaster, war and famine fell on them. We see this in Jer. 44:11-14. This practice was highly criticized by the prophet Jeremiah.

Today religious people are praying to statues made of plaster and plastic. The one who intercedes to the queen of heaven is idolizing just as the people of Judah did. No other name can be called upon to save or to heal than Jesus. He is the only mediator between God and man as seen in 1 Tim. 2:5. Otherwise it is idolatry.

Marialogy

During the fifth century, devotion to Mary started to appear. In 1854, Pope Pius IX declared the dogma of the Immaculate Conception. He encouraged people to worship Mary. The church, at this time, held a very powerful influence over the people. Statues, pictures, icons, etc. of the Savior's mother were located throughout the churches. People were encouraged to pray to the statue, using rosaries and asking her to intervene on their behalf.

Occasional appearances of Mary have been reported. She asks the faithful to say rosaries to her so that she can intervene to Jesus on their behalf. (First appearance of rosaries was in 1090. Official adoption by the Church of Rome was in the seventh century).

However, when this being appears representing Mary and asks the people to worship her, you can be sure that this is not from God. This being is receiving the adoration instead of the son of Mary. It doesn't say, "pray to my Son," but "pray to me". She wants to be worshiped.

Mary, having been raised in the Judean religion and knowing the Torah, would have known about the second commandment of God in Exodus 20:4 which revealed that no one was to make any graven image or idol or worship them. Only our Almighty God is to be worshiped.

These false apparitions, masquerading as Mary, ask to be prayed to and worshiped. However, Ex. 20:3 clearly states that we are not to worship any other God.

Power that only belongs to God is attributed to Mary. People are even told to pray to Mary to get into heaven. By praying to Mary religious people focus their attention on her instead of Jesus. In John 14:7 we learn differently. *"Jesus said unto him, I am the way, the truth, and the life: no man cometh unto the Father but by me."* **KJV** This fallacy has led many astray and given false hope. Jesus Christ is the only true intercessor.

Jesus was the one who had the power to do miracles, not his mother. See what Jesus had to say in Luke 11:27,28: *" As he was speaking, a woman in the crowd called out, "God bless your mother -----the womb from which you came, and the breasts that gave you suck!" He replied, "Yes, but even more blessed are all who hear the word of God and put it into practice."* LB Where was her special power? Nowhere in the Bible is she described as having any.

In John 2:1-11, we see Mary telling the servants to do whatever Jesus told them to do. Jesus performed the miracles, not Mary. He was the one who shed His blood to cover our sin, not his mother.

In Luke 10:17, the apostles were so excited that they could cast devils out of people using the powerful name of Jesus. They were not using the name of Mary but that of Jesus.

On the cross Jesus was concerned about the welfare of his mother. I presume that Joseph was now dead for he was never referred to afterwards in the scriptures.

The Bible has no trace of Joseph at the scene of the cross when Jesus was crucified. When Mary and her children followed Jesus when He was ministering, Joseph was never there as the scriptures reveal in John 2:12; Mark 3:31-35; Luke 19:21. Jesus turned to the disciple John, whom He loved, and put her in his care in John 19:26. I do not believe John was to take her under his roof for her other sons were alive.

However, at this time Jesus' brothers did not believe that He was the Messiah according to John 7:3-10; and Matt. 12:46-47. Jesus was more concerned about her being persecuted for her belief.

In Acts 1:13-14, Mary was in the upper room with her children and the apostles to receive the baptism of the Holy Spirit. The last thing she wanted was to take away the attention from her son. We are to respect her as the mother of Jesus but not to worship her.

Throughout the rest of the Bible there is no more mention of Mary the mother of Jesus. Acts 4:12 says ***"Jesus is the only name to call upon to answer your prayers."***

Signs and Wonders

John 4:48 "Except you see signs and wonders, ye will not believe." KJV

As in Jesus' day, so today, people are wanting to see signs, demonstrations of the miraculous or revelations of future happenings (see John 6:30; Mark 8:12; Luke 11:16; and John 2:18). Instead of developing their faith through prayer and Bible study, they are turning to astrology or the occult looking for God. Believers try to build their faith by worshiping other gods. Countless become lukewarm when, after numerous intercessory prayers, they receive no answer.

Satan is a liar and he is able to show counterfeit signs but a curse will also accompany them as 2 Th. 2: 9-12 tells us.

How can we discern for ourselves if the signs are from Satan? Study the scriptures. Anything contrary to the Bible or written word is not of God but from the deceiver. The only thing the counterfeit wants to do is destroy the fellowship between the Heavenly Father and His children. He wants to bring destruction, gloom, sorrow, grief, misery and depression.

Those ignorant of the Scriptures will be singled out. Innocent victims will be drawn into the occult because of a lack of knowledge. Satan hates good people and his motive is to destroy them. He is jealous of the worship and adoration we give to our wonderful Father. His tactics are to steal the glory from our Lord by getting God's children involved in witchcraft. Then he receives the adulation and power over the lives of Christians.

There is a principle in Deut. 28 that those who break the rules of scripture will inherit the curse of the law. There will be a legacy of misery, sorrow, distress and calamity that is the result of opening the door of sin to these familiar spirits.

In Acts 19:19, those who became Christians and had been involved in the occult and witchcraft repented and brought all their magical arts books to burn them.

I have seen people who were involved in the occult set free after they burned thousands of dollars in books, tapes and C.D.'s. These burnt items were about Astrology, Parapsychology, Transcendental, Meditation, Rebirth Yourself and so on. Praise the Lord!

A curse is also brought upon the person who prays to other gods. The first commandment of God stated in Ex. 20:4 is, *"Thou shalt have no other gods before me."*

In the religion in which I was raised, the second commandment of God was taken away at the council of Trent (1545-1563). A law of the Ten Commandments was subtracted. We were asked to worship other gods such as apparitions of those who died having supported worthy causes. We were taught to venerate Saints, loved ones who had died... This means another law was added to the scriptures. Rev. 22:18-19 declares, *"And I solemnly declare to everyone who reads this book (Bible): If anyone adds anything to what is written here, God shall add to him the plagues described in this book. And if anyone subtracts any part of these prophecies, God shall take away his share in the Tree of Life, and in the Holy City just described,"* LB

Our heavenly Father would rather give abundantly to his children. When you go to other idols such as images, statues or mediums you will get an answer but a curse will accompany it.

Go directly to Jesus through the Holy Spirit and your prayer request will be heard. Only Jesus can answer your petitions. He is the only one who shed His blood to cover your sin and only His shed blood will erase it.

In John 16:23 Jesus said to start asking in His Name and the Father would give it to you. 1 Tim. 2:5 states *"For there is only one God and one mediator between God and men, the man Christ Jesus." KJV*

Mildred's Story

I was born in a family with many children. My parents were very religious so I learned to pray at a very young age. My mother would always say, "Remember, if you do something wrong, even if I am not there, Jesus is always watching you." I had older brothers who were sexually molesting me.

I didn't tell my precious mother for in my little child's mind I knew I was going to hurt her and she would be disappointed in me. So I kept this terrible secret to myself. I felt so ashamed for deep down inside I knew it was wrong. Every night I prayed that my brothers would leave home so they would stop molesting me and I would not feel so guilty.

I left home at the age of thirteen to find work to help in providing for the family. I could not understand why men were always making sexual advances toward me. Today I know why. I had a sexual curse of perversion on me as a result of the incest.

I got married very young. My husband's father was an alcoholic and because of his drinking lost his business to bankruptcy. My husband's family never had any money and the curse followed the bloodline. My husband lost his business to bankruptcy and we never had any money. Our son also lost his business to bankruptcy and never had any money. The curse of alcoholism through my father-in-law jumped one generation; our son became an alcoholic. The curse came down, and what the father sowed, the son and the grandson reaped, suffering the same fate.

My father-in-law was a womanizer and the curse jumped one generation resulting in the grandson being a womanizer. What the grandfather enjoyed, the grandson is paying the price for his inability to maintain lasting relationships.

Eleven months after my marriage I had a beautiful little girl who died a few days after birth. I was devastated and though I never cried, a terrible rage controlled me. In my anger I would be cruel to my husband. I knew he loved me but he was working seven days a week and I rarely saw him.

I started to work to get us out of debt. I had three other children after we lost our first child and I had the responsibility of raising our children alone since my husband was never at home. This caused bigger fights between my husband and myself. Since my husband was never there for me I grew cold toward him. I was so lonely.

I was looking for things to fill the void. My nephew started to talk to me about a book of T. Lubsang Rampas. I didn't know this was witchcraft. I started to experiment with this newfound control. I had authority in commanding these powers and I was fascinated. Now I felt needed.

I showed others how to do levitation and astral projection. This frightened me so much I never tried to project myself again. I never realized I was dealing with the occult. On top of this my husband's business was glorifying the work of darkness. Often magicians were brought in by my husband's work and we would go and listen to them.

Unknown to me a door was opened for demons to begin their work of destruction in our lives. The curse was already there from my husband's father because of the alcoholic syndrome and now another door was opened for Satan to bring ravage and destruction.

Since my husband was not making enough money to pay our bills I started to work to help make both ends meet. But it's like there was a bag and the money disappeared as fast as it came in. The thief was at our door.

My husband wanted to keep his business at all cost. It didn't matter if the children and I suffered the consequences. I was now living daily in anger and rage. I gave him the money I earned and I never knew what he did with it. He would never tell me what he paid or how it disappeared. He had no wisdom and a spirit of confusion blinded me.

As a people-pleasing person, always wanting approval, I even boarded his father for ten years. His own children would not even take him in or care for him. The thank you note I got was that he molested my daughter while under our roof. When I discovered the abuse, I asked my husband to throw him out of the house but he refused. I packed my suitcase and as I was leaving he told me he was going to put his dad in a nursing home. Even so, that didn't help our marriage much.

The children grew up without a good role model as their father was more an absentee father and their mother was infuriated with anger all the time. Our home was a battleground. When I wanted to discipline my children and train them in the ways of the Lord my husband would always tell them the opposite. I wanted to raise them spiritually but he would tell them otherwise. I could have killed him. That was how furious I had become over the years.

Then my daughter became pregnant and left to live with her boyfriend. An older woman sexually abused my oldest son. When my son told me about it I was devastated.

When the boys left I asked my husband to choose between his business and me. He chose his business and while he was working, I packed my things and left. I was hurt, feeling unloved and unwanted and I kept all the rejection and the pain buried inside of me.

I went to live with my sister who tried to help me in so many ways. I started to work but would have nothing to do with my husband when he would call and want to speak with me. I suffered a small heart attack while away from home. Again my sister cared for me and loved me.

While away from home my children never phoned or inquired about me. That hurt the most. Since I had never said a word of what was going on between their father and myself they blamed me for everything. The wound in my heart was too strong to bear. I finally let go one day and cried all the tears I had held inside for so many years.

Then I found the Lord. I accepted Him as my Savior and repented of my sins. I became a Christian. I had found Jesus! The curse of witchcraft was broken. I still didn't want to have anything to do with my spouse. My husband wanted so much to have me back that he even started to go to church on his own. He was willing to do anything to have me home again. He also gave his life to God. I returned home.

I went ahead of God and started a business of my own. It lasted for sometime, and because I was not making enough money to pay my bills, I had to close the shop with the added bills.

Before I had left my husband we had co-signed a loan with our son to pay for a business of his own. Because my husband was also a people-pleaser, he coaxed me to sign. Since I didn't want to be the bad guy I signed also. I have regretted dearly this poor judgment.

My son went bankrupt after a while because of a lack of wisdom. The curse of bankruptcy was repeated in our son's life. Since he could not pay us back we had to declare bankruptcy, also. The beautiful home which I had worked so hard to help pay for was gone. Again that didn't help our marriage since I had been against signing for our son in the first place.

Because Satan had a breeding ground for all these thieves in our life (he stole our peace, our health, our money), he left us with a spirit of broken marriage and family breakup as our inheritance.

My oldest son got divorced after a few years of marriage and he became an alcoholic. What a tragedy. It was like every curse of Deut. 28:15-65 was falling on our heads.

Then, I met a lady who has the gift of discerning of spirits. I had intensive deliverance. I am regaining back every legal hold and ground that Satan stole from me. I was set free of many spirits. These included: witchcraft, the occult, rebellion, rage, sexual abuse, mental torment, stubbornness, hate, rejection, unloved, unwanted, temper tantrum, screaming, yelling, madness, jealousy, competition, envy, uncontrollable rage, falsely accused, no wisdom, broken heart, pain, blue anger, violent anger, weak mind.... My master is now the Lord Jesus Christ, my Savior and He redeemed me from the curse of the law. I can say I have victory over the attacks Satan tries to send my way. My eyes are opened spiritually to his deceiving ways.

Am I completely set free from his daily conniving ways? I don't think so, but with the blood of Jesus Christ I claim victory daily. The battle is not over, for we are living on the earth where he surrounds us daily.

Now before I get up in the morning, I bind every strategy that he builds in the middle of the night in the precious name of Jesus. I place a hedge of protection over, around and under my house, my husband, my children, my grandchildren, and myself. By binding his powers before I get up, he is powerless to attack any members of my family. Alleluia!

I wish I would have known all this when I got married. I would have foiled his plan before he had a chance to destroy us and cause all the misery he has tormented us with. Praise God for the ministry of discerning of spirits. We can have victory over the powers of darkness.

Author's note: Please teach your children about the damage that the power of witchcraft can cause. Do not let the thief steal one day of their precious life. If you don't teach them then somebody will influence them to touch these powers and they will suffer terribly. Like Moses who warn the Israelites in Deut. 4:9, *"Only be careful, and watch yourselves closely so that you do not forget the things your eyes have seen or let them slip from your heart as long as you live. Teach them to your children and to their children after them"*. NIV

Chapter 7

Psychic Powers and Psychic Prayers

Psychic Healing

A lady approached me for deliverance. She shared how her husband had a stroke and could only speak two words. She was devastated and wanted help. She revealed that they were seeing a psychic healer once a week. I asked if her pastor was aware of these visits. She stated that he was not only aware but expressed that, "if he was in the same position he would do the same thing."

I explained to her that as a Christian she was not to see a psychic healer because their power was not from God. "Oh," she said, "this is the same gift of healing as the gifts of healing in the Bible."

I asked her how the psychic prayed when they saw him. She replied, "He doesn't pray. We talk about the weather."

"But how do you get healed?"

She replied, "By a special power inside of him which he was born with. He heals you by touching you or looking at you."

I proceeded to explain to her the difference between the gifts of healing that were psychic and gifts of healing that belonged to God.

In Acts 19:13-16, the seven sons of Sceva tried to imitate Paul by using spells or incantations to exorcise or heal in the name of Jesus. We read what followed in verse 15, *"And the evil spirits answered and said, Jesus I know and Paul I know; but who are you?"* The spirits overcame them and wounded them. They found out the hard way that spirituality doesn't mix with psychic powers.

Examples of psychic powers we see today are: hypnotism, fortune telling, astrology, healing by the power of the mind, seeking false interpretation of dreams, casting spells through amulets and charms, divination, telepathy, and other unusual para-psychological abilities.

All who reject the Word of the scriptures and try to heal by using these powers are not of God, for it is only God who has the power to heal and He heals us through the shed blood of His Son, Jesus Christ. I Peter 2:24 speaks of Jesus when it says, *"Who his own self bare our sins in his own body on the tree, that we, being dead to sins, should live unto righteousness: by whose stripes ye are healed."* KJV

Some, like this woman, innocently get involved in these forbidden practices because of not being grounded in the Bible and also because the church fails to teach them. The only way Christians can guard against these deceiving methods is to study the Word to know the difference between God's way and Satan's lies.

In contrast to psychic healings, we see in 1 Cor. chapters 12, 13 and 14, the gifts God has given to His children. The scriptures describe for us the functions of the many gifts of the spirit. Healing and wonders take place when God imparts these gifts to the believers. He equips them with wisdom, knowledge and discerning of spirits to guide them. God, through the Holy Spirit and our renewed mind, performs the inspired manifestations of these gifts. Because of the shed blood of Jesus Christ the gifts are made visible and edify the believers. As the recipients of these precious gifts we are to remain faithful to use the gifts as God enables (1 Tim. 4:14).

The Origin of Psychic Powers

Let me try to explain the origin of psychic powers. To do so we have to go back to the beginning of creation and take a look at what it might have been like.

In Gen. 1:26-28 before Adam sinned, God gave him supremacy over all living things. God trusted him and empowered him to rule, care for, protect from the enemy, and have dominion over the fish of the sea, the birds of the air and over every living thing that moved on the earth. Man was the crowning glory of God's creation and I believe God endowed man with extraordinary powers.

Adam must have been highly intelligent for the scriptures tell us in Gen. 2:19, ***"And out of the ground the Lord God formed every beast of the field, and every fowl of the air; and brought them unto Adam to see what he would call them: and whatsoever Adam called every living creature, that was the name thereof."*** **KJV** He must have had exceptional ability to name all the animals God brought to him. Today a person needs a dictionary to remember all their names but instantly, Adam had the wisdom to identify them.

The scriptures tell us that there were only two people to take care of the entire garden. Can you image the vastness of the Garden of Eden? Yet God expected

Adam to do the job. He must have equipped Adam with great ability to perform such a task. Perhaps he could be transported bodily from one place to another like Philip in Acts 8:39 and distance was no problem.

In John 6:21, the minute Jesus stepped into the boat it immediately reached the shore. It was perhaps the way Adam and Eve cared for the immensity of the garden. They were in contact with God daily as seen in Gen. 3:8.

In any case, Adam must have had phenomenal ability for he had dominion over the works of God's hand as the scriptures reveal in Gen. 1:26 *" And God said, Let us make man in our image, after our likeness: and let them have dominion over the fowl of the air, and over the cattle, and over all the earth, and over every creeping thing that creepeth upon the earth.* KJV

These other verses will reveal what are the works of God's hands in Ps. 8:3-9, Heb. 1:10, Isa. 45:12, Isa. 48:13, Ps. 102:25.

Before Adam sinned and was cursed, life was much different from what we know today. The earth was perfect before the fall. But when the curse came, all things were affected and even the weather became a problem. The animals also, were affected as a result of Adam's disobedience.

Before Adam disobeyed, there was no violence or killing among the animals for they were gentle. But after the curse, they became antagonistic and aggressive. After Adam's fall, the curse of hard labor and sweating came on him as we can see in Gen. 3:19. What Adam could do with ease and great ability before the curse, he now had to work at by the sweat of his brow.

Can you imagine the anger and the rage that must have been in Adam when he realized he had no more Godly power?

Before the fall, Adam was so healthy that he was to live forever for neither the curse of death nor ill health existed. That came after the fall. Rom. 6:23 tells us that the wages of sin is death. Both death and sin originated when Adam disobeyed God and are now propagated by Satan. When God said to go and multiply, Eve was to have children without pain. Part of Eve's curse was to bear children in great pain.

As a result of their disobedience, they were forced to leave the Garden. The scriptures tell us in Gen. 3:22, 23, if they had stayed in the Garden they would have had access to the tree of life and lived forever physically as sinners. So they had to leave the Garden and eventually die physically.

The last enemy to be conquered is the curse of death as seen in 1 Cor. 15:26 and Rev. 21:4.

Now you may ask, "What happened to Adam's supernatural powers?" I believe when Adam and Eve fell and the curse came on the earth, they lost the supernatural ability of God working through them. When they fell, their spirits were no longer alive. They died spiritually. They could no longer have the same fellowship with God and He (God) could no longer work through man's spirit for it became dormant. They were no longer plugged in to God, the power source of their spiritual power. The power was still available but now it was cursed.

And now it is Satan who desires to expand this soul (psyche) power. For this reason all who develop it (soul power) cannot avoid being contacted and used by evil spirits.

The only way man can restore his fellowship with God is through Our Redeemer and Savior Jesus Christ, by being born again. He receives, at that moment, spiritual life.

Here is another source of psychic power.

Witchcraft

What is witchcraft? It is a supernatural power acquired by contact with evil spirits. It is a power that comes from a psychic force within. Many who participate in this kind of healing really believe that their gift comes from God.

I know a man who has the power to stop the flow of blood. He says that if a person is bleeding then they only have to think of him and the blood flow will stop.

If this healing gift was of God it would be done in the name of Jesus Christ through the power of the Holy Spirit. Yet, this man cannot speak two words without swearing and blaspheming the name of God. He hates, holds grudges or seeks revenge against anyone who criticizes him. He shared how he puts curses of death on anyone who has done him wrong.

Another man had a gift of fixing broken bones. Behind the scenes this renowned person was a pedophile; a spirit of pedophilia was controlling him. He abused many and no one dared to speak up for fear of not being believed. Tremendous damage, which was unsuspected and went undetected in the lives of these individuals, was done for it gave the enemy a door to enter to control them with spirits of perversion.

Did these powers of healing come from God? Would God operate this way? No! This man was using his psychic or soul power. These types of powers can be revisited upon the next generation when ancestors, who were involved in the occult, had never been released from this power by faith in Jesus Christ. The ability to perform these healings with a psychic power from within then comes down to the next generation as a result of contact with the powers of darkness.

Satan wants to raise that soul power within so that he can manipulate the victims. When you attend a meeting where they tell you to contact your inner quest, your energy connection, the magnetic alignment of the charkas or to rebirth yourself, do not do it. All those who develop these soul powers are contacted and used of Satan for he is the one behind these soul forces. These things originated and are also propagated by the devil. They are not of God.

These are not new psychic powers that are taught today. They are old Satanic practices taught under different new names. These magical abilities were far advanced in the Old Testament as we can read in Exodus chapters 7-8.

Real deliverance or healing is done when one has a special anointing of God to operate in these gifts. The gift of healing is a supernatural power to heal all kinds of sickness and disease without the help of medication. It is not done by a power that was inherited by the grandfather or was handed down by being born the seventh in the family. It is done by or in the name of Jesus Christ, who shed His blood so you can be healed.

Here is another form of witchcraft.

Psychic Prayer

I will give you another form of psychic power. This is psychic prayer. I went to a prayer meeting one night and a Christian lady seated behind me asked if I needed prayer. I was surprised that she had detected this. I proceeded to explain to her how one of my children was being persecuted. She emphatically said she would intercede for my child.

I went home thankful to God that another person was praying also. What happened the next three days baffled me! Instead of my young one being released from the oppression it got worse. Now I was really crying out to God for help asking, "Lord what is going on?"

The Holy Spirit revealed psychic prayer. That is when I learned for the first time about such a prayer. You see, the moment this woman started to pray for my child she directed her prayer toward my child instead of sending her prayer toward God. My young one was in such turmoil that he couldn't sleep. She was using the strength of her soul power to control his mind by prayer. This is witchcraft. She was using her psychic means to move the condition around my offspring. I believe this person was very innocent and didn't know the damage she was doing.

I broke every psychic prayer and psychic power on my child in the name of Jesus and the persecution stopped right away. He became peaceful.

When a hurting one asks an intercessor for prayer and when he/she starts to pray and they send prayer by concentrating all their mental energy toward that person and not praying to God, then their prayer is a psychic one. This is what we call mind control.

How many Christians pray and intercede for others and, through ignorance, send their soul power behind their prayer to control the circumstances of another one?

How many churches are under this kind of witchcraft-controlled prayer? The one receiving this kind of prayer will be in such oppression that some even get sick. It taught me a lesson: to beware of those who pray for my family or me.

I will give you another example. I went to this little church while on a trip. As the service proceeded three people got up and one by one started to reveal what God was saying to them. The Holy Spirit checked me in my spirit. I whispered to my prayer partner, "Do these people realize that these exhortations are not from God? These revelations are of the flesh."

She replied, "They do this all the time."

I was appalled, for even the pastor didn't know the difference between what was a psychic prayer and what was a spiritual one. The Holy Spirit revealed that a spirit of divination attached to clairvoyance was used in this church and nobody knew the difference. I was upset to say the least. How will they discern when a false prophet comes in their midst? Or even an antichrist? This verse came into my mind: Matt. 24:24, *"For false Christs and false prophets will arise, and will show great signs and wonders, so as to deceive and lead astray, if possible, even the elect (God's chosen ones)." AMB* It is important to pray to have discernment in these last days. Pray to receive wisdom from the Lord (James 1:5). Learn to recognize His voice and therefore being able to discern what is from the enemy.

A lady called me one day and she was very upset. She was sharing that every time she went to church, a seminar, or a convention prophecies were prayed for everybody else but they always bypassed her. She asked, "Doesn't God love me or care for me? Why are so many receiving prophecies and words of knowledge, and I don't receive any?" She was heartbroken, discouraged and feeling rejected by God.

While talking to her, the Holy Spirit gave me a word of knowledge. I told her she didn't have to receive any prophecies from anybody else; she was receiving them directly from God. That was even better. She was encouraged and her spirit lightened up.

I will try to explain why this is happening. If a person was involved in the occult, astrology, esoteric philosophies, witchcraft, etc. before they became a Christian, they developed a supernatural ability to see beyond the fifth sense.

After they become born again they will innocently use their soul power, thinking it is the Holy Spirit. When that psychic power is brought to the surface, a spirit of divination and clairvoyance is the one revealing some of these exhortations, prophecies or dreams.

Because these innocent ones have not been delivered of their psychic soul power, they are not aware that they are using a power of the soul to reveal a word of knowledge or a prophecy. They think this is the Holy Spirit talking to their spirit. But all the time it is an evil spirit. This is why many false prophecies are being revealed.

These people have not learned the difference between a psychic prophecy and a prophecy that comes from the Holy Spirit. They have to be delivered from occult practices by binding every soul power and soul force that doesn't come from God. They will then be clean vessels for divine revelation.

A special friend of mine wrote me this letter. She was very puzzled and offended in a prayer meeting that she had attended. Here is an excerpt of her letter.

"I went to a convention to hear an evangelist. I was told he was a prophet of God. The service began with singing. Then the pastor started to preach. I agreed with everything he said. He spoke the truth but one thing I noticed was that he never used his Bible and didn't quote any scripture.

Then the collection was taken during the service. Only it was done in a way I've never seen it done before. There was no collection plate passed. The evangelist stood in front with envelopes in his hands. He said 'I believe there are twenty people present tonight who could give one hundred dollars each'.

When no one answered he kept asking over and over again. He told the people that he believed those who already had the stamp of the anti-Christ on them were those who were bound by their money, and that was the reason they were not giving. He manipulated them with guilt until someone raised their hand. Then he personally went to those people and handed them an envelope.

When they were finished writing their cheques, he went to pick up their offerings and shake their hands praying for God to bless them a hundred fold. He warned the people when he picked up their envelopes to be sure that they had put in the amount of money they had committed to because he could very well open their envelope right there in front of them to see what was inside.

I was horrified. Then he said, 'I believe there are three people present tonight who can give one thousand dollars each'. When one lifted her hand she received a long prophecy when he took the envelope. (The one's who gave one hundred dollars had a small prophecy). The only blessing these people received was his handshake.

I verbalized my disagreement to this kind of collection to my friend beside me. But I was told that if I had a problem with this then it was my problem.

The thought that struck me was, is it only those who can afford one hundred or one thousand dollars that can receive an abundance of blessing? What about all those who can only afford five dollars? Does that mean they only receive five dollars worth of blessings? I was shattered. Praying I asked God, 'Please Lord I don't want to judge but show me if this is of you?'

Some time later God enlightened me through Matt. 6:1-4, *"Take care! Don't do your good deeds publicly, to be admired, for then you will lose the reward from your Father in heaven. When you give a gift to a beggar, don't shout about it as the hypocrites do--- blowing trumpets in the synagogues and streets to call attention to their acts of charity! I tell you in all earnestness, they have received all the reward they will ever get. But when you do a kindness to someone, do it secretly---don't tell your left hand what your right hand is doing. And your Father who knows all secrets will reward you."* **LB**

Were these prophesies of God? I don't think so. This was a psychic way to gather money for his greediness. Were the Christians able to differentiate between this man and a true prophet of God? Very few were able to and the rest ran to him with dollar bills to buy a prophecy that didn't come from God but from his psychic power within. The people were being fleeced of their hard earned money. And many were hurt since they believed God had spoken to them when all the time it was a lie.

A man revealed to me a prophecy that was given to him, telling him that he was to have a big ministry. This information went to his head and as a result of pride he quit a good paying job to stay home to prepare for his divine appointment.

His wife was working to support the family and it didn't take long for the finances to vanish. Having discerned that this prophecy was not of God she was angry. She tried to explain to him that when God calls you to start a ministry He equips and provides you with spiritual power, gives you wisdom to learn to listen to His voice and know when a prophecy is given in the flesh and when it is given in the Spirit. Her husband was not able to discern these things.

She had more wisdom spiritually for she knew the difference. No amount of pleading and trying to reason with him mattered. He went ahead and quit his job.

After waiting on God for a long period of time with no ministry opening up for him, he realized this was a false prophecy and went back to work. He is a much happier man today. There was much needless suffering.

When people are given a word of knowledge in front of a group or congregation, a spirit of self-importance can enter and they can forget about testing the words they receive against God's Word. They don't ask God to confirm the word they received by two or three witnesses.

The Bible clearly states to test or to examine prophecies given according to 2 Tim. 2:15 *" Study to shew thyself approved unto God, a workman that needeth not to be ashamed, rightly dividing the word of truth."* KJV Did it confirm what God had already spoken to your spirit? This is a second witness. Is this word prophetic for the future, to take place in maybe five, ten or fifteen years? Is there a waiting period for God to prepare you for the work ahead? Someone who, never having heard the prophecy, will sometimes make the same statement and confirm the word. Then the word will have been tested. We cannot jump to conclusions right away and say, "Oh, God has spoken to me and I must obey right away."

Many haven't confirmed the spoken word that was given to them and have lost their own family or years of savings. You must exercise common sense and pray to receive wisdom to test the word.

It took Abraham and Sarah thirteen years to have the son that God had promised. They didn't have the patience to wait but went ahead and wanted to help God a little. Their disobedience and sin brought needless suffering.

Joseph was tested thirteen years before God could use him. We must learn to be patient and wait upon God to confirm any prophecy or word of knowledge that is given. Luke 1:37 tells us, *"For every promise of God shall surely come true."* **LB**

Before reading the next story ask God to shield you and protect you. Cover your thoughts, your mind, your will and your emotions with the blood of Jesus. I pray the Lord will enlighten and give you understanding to warn loved ones who are involved in psychic power. This is the story of a woman, who was involved with familiar spirits and found freedom.

Heavenly Father I bow in worship before you. I cover myself with the blood of Jesus Christ. I surrender myself to you and ask that you protect my mind, my will and my emotions while reading this testimony. I now close the door of every spirit that could oppress me right now in the name of Jesus Christ. Amen

Abigail's Path to Freedom

"I was raised in a family where I had good religious parents. Later on in life I was married to a wonderful husband who I dearly loved and we had two children. My forefathers were of Indian descent. I was attracted to the paranormal and I became heavily involved in the esoteric courses and upgraded to the occult movement. I Tim. 4:1 tells us, *"Now the Spirit speaketh expressly, that in the latter times some shall depart from the faith, giving heed to seductive spirits, and doctrines of devils." KJV* (Author's note: For a list of these courses see the list mentioned earlier on Familiar Spirit Involvement in chapter 6.)

I was born with a tremendous ability to predict the future and I enjoyed the power I was receiving, unknowingly from Satan. I had three hundred students at my mercy. They would not make any major decisions without consulting me because of my psychic powers. I was like a god to them. I traveled around the world and recruited many members. Some, to increase their satanic powers, offered to pay millions of dollars to sleep with me. I Cor. 6:16 tells us, *"What? Know you not that he which is joined to an harlot is one body? For two, saith he, shall be one flesh." KJV (*See also Luke 22:3; John 13:27) (Religious people are very ignorant of the tactics of the powers of darkness when sexual intercourse or adultery is done outside of marriage with someone other than their mate.) I really thought I was helping others. I was gathering a following into Satan's kingdom.

When I was a Rosicrucian, I followed the Satanic calendar. I really thought this movement was spiritual. How my eyes were blinded. I gradually upgraded to become a sorceress and I followed the same calendar. There are four major festivities in this calendar. Between the 21-22 of June we celebrated the summer Solstice Feast Day. This was the day the sun god had the most power and the followers tried to increase their occult powers.

The next celebration was between the 21-22 of September, the Autumn Equinox Feast Day, which is when night and day are of equal length and spells are cast for balance or equality. The feminist movement, wanting equal status with men, would be a good example of the type of spells and charms that were cast during this festival. It was also filled with sexual rituals.

Between the 21-22 of December was the Solstice Feast Day commemorating the rebirth of the sun god. It was also celebrated with a sexual ritual and a feast. This was to receive more demonic power and advance in grade.

Between the 21-22 of March was Equinox Feast Day that included a sexual ritual with animals (the sin of bestiality was punishable by death according to Ex. 22:19; Lev. 20:15; Deut. 27:21). The one thing the followers want is to worship their god, Satan. They are also controlled by fear. Looking back it amazes me how humans can degrade themselves so.

We had other days of celebration on the ritual calendar. One of the high points of the festivities was the very intense Halloween night. This was one of the biggest days of celebration for witches. I can assure you that when I was involved we had parties where sorcerers and sorceresses would talk to and invoke evil spirits. On Halloween night, cats and dogs would disappear to be used in blood sacrifices to Satan. In fact, it is a day dedicated to blood sacrifices and sexual activities.

Since Satan wants to get involved even with innocent children, he uses this day to entice them. Seemingly an innocent practice, the children see no harm in pretending to be evil by dressing up in evil costumes.

From year to year the costumes and masks are getting scarier. Common costumes are monsters, skeletons, phantoms, etc.

What they don't know is Halloween began as a festival of the Samhain to the old Celtic god of death that was practiced 2000 years ago. This feast started with the druids. They would dress like animals and wear animal headdresses. Some legends say that the soul of a wicked person who had died was condemned to live in an animal for twelve months.

Others believed that these spirits haunted the living. To keep the spirits away from people's home they would light bonfires. The custom of those days was also to prepare food and put outside the door to give a treat to these wicked spirits. If the spirit came back to the house and didn't find food he would put a curse on the house and all kinds of bad luck would happen to the family. This is probably where the trick or treat tradition came from.

Halloween is considered by the sorcerers and sorceresses to be the best time of the year to contact evil spirits. They say that untold numbers of evil spirits are let loose on the earth that night.

Can you imagine the evil that is let loose when all those who are involved in Satanism are doing their incantations to contact evil spirits in combined forces? No wonder they are roaming the earth on that evening.

Some of the other holidays that are celebrated to increase their Satanic or occult power to control others include:

1. The seventh of January, for blood sacrifices to Satan. Here an animal might be killed or a person

would cut himself and everybody had to drink the blood.

2. The seventeenth of January is the celebration of sexual promiscuity. Everyone has to have sexual relations with someone other than their married partner. Satan loves this kind of perverted orgy and debauchery. Do you wonder why AIDS is spreading so much today?

3. The second of February the followers must have sexual relations with children. Some abuse their own children. What utter depravation. When a person abuses a defenseless child sexually we call it pedophilia; we call it sexual abuse. These people have an evil eye and they are so corrupted by their allegiance to Satan that their deceitful desire of perversion for more Satanic power has blinded their mind. Their heart is so harden they are ready to offer their seed as an offering to the one who is destroying them. What wickedness. In Matt. 18:6 Jesus tells us, *'But whoso shall offend one of these little ones which believe in me, it were better for him that a millstone were hanged about his neck, and that he were drowned in the depth of the sea'.* **KJV**

4. The twenty-fifth of February is the communion celebration. On that day all the followers have to drink blood and urine. How disgusting!

5. The twentieth of March is the celebration of bestiality where followers engage in sexual relations with animals. How horrible the perversion and degradation of man and how his

corrupted mind can bring him lower than an animal.

6. From the twenty-sixth of April to the first of May there is again a celebration of sexual rituals for higher power.

7. From the first of July to the third of August another sexual ritual is celebrated. All come together and perform all kinds of ritualistic sexual abuse that will show they belong to Satan. It can get very corrupt. Orgies of all kind take place during this time span.

8. The seventh of September a human baby is traditionally sacrificed to Satan. The child is usually the offspring of a young woman of the Coven group who they previously impregnated. Only Satan can have his followers perform such abominations.

Usually these ceremonies include alcohol consumption and drugs to help desensitize the followers against the atrocities being performed. In their meeting they also put spirits of charms, spells, and curses of death on people. This is not an exhaustive list of all the ceremonies celebrated by witches. However, it should help you to understand the evil they practice.

Many unsuspectingly become involved in the occult. Many people who travel to other countries bring back masks and statuettes as decorations for their homes. They do this not realizing that many of these artifacts have already been dedicated to Satan and will attack their minds and bring havoc to their families.

Once involved in the occult it is difficult to break away. These are dangerous people. If someone disagrees with the rituals, they are in danger of losing their life. If someone of a different sect tries to intervene in another's ritual, their life also is in danger.

I could go on and on but I have shared numerous tactics (esoteric and parapsychology course) that the enemy uses to get individuals involved and keep followers in his vicious power and circle. But please know that there is hope.

One day I was so privileged to hear about the Gospel. I heard of the blood sacrifice that Jesus made 2000 years ago. He didn't have to ritualistically die or shed His blood over and over again for the forgiveness of my sin. Hebrews 9:28 says, *"So Christ was once offered to bear the sins of many: and unto them that look for him shall he appear the second time without sin unto salvation."* **KJV** He paid the penalty once and for all on the cross so I could be set free from the oppression of the enemy. I accepted Jesus Christ as my personal Savior. Alleluia, Alleluia. I renounced and broke every involvement that I had had with the power of darkness and I wanted to live daily for Christ. The gift of discerning of spirits through the power of Jesus Christ delivered me from the bondage of Satanism. I told Satan to get out of my house and my family in the name of Jesus. I thank God daily that through His grace and His mercy I was set free from all this corruption. Though my sins were crimson, Jesus, through His shed blood on the cross has set me free and has washed me white as snow as revealed in Isaiah 1:18 where it says, *"Come now, and let us reason together, saith the Lord: though your sins* *be as scarlet, they shall be as white as snow; though they be red like crimson, they shall be as wool.*" **KJV** What a wonderful Savior and forgiving Father we have.

Are you afraid of these dates mentioned above? Don't be, for Satan lost his powers at the cross and he has none except what you give him through fear. You can become a prayer warrior and an intercessor to help break the power of darkness on those evil calendar days.

If you are involved in the esoteric courses, occult, sorcery, astrology, palm reading, predicting the future through the stars, necromancy, etc. you might think that these practices are innocent. Don't kid yourself. The enemy, like a roaring lion, is roaming the earth trying to get another innocent victim in his net (James 4:7). And when you get involved, he will control you by fears. In Hosea 4:6 it says, "*My people are destroyed for lack of knowledge.*" **KJV**

Take the time to study our guide, the Holy Bible. This is a gift that God has given to us for direction. Teach your children while they are young so they will not be recruited into the enemy's stronghold. It is through the wisdom you will receive from this Book that He will protect you from the path of destruction and all the lies of the enemy. I know, since I have been redeemed from the curse that was on me because of my involvement in Satanism. But now I will keep on praising the holy name of Jesus because, as Ps. 118:6 says, "*The Lord is on my side; I will not fear: what can man do unto me?*" **KJV**

Chapter 8

Abnormal Sex

In the beginning when God created the animals and man He said that everything was good and pleasant. Gen. 1:3 states, *"And God saw every thing that he had made, and, behold it was very good. And the evening and the morning were the sixth day." KJV*

He also gave the command to go and be fruitful and multiply. When God said to Adam and Eve to go and multiply and replenish the earth that meant mating together for reproduction. This was to be done through sexual intercourse or copulation.

God created sex and the beautiful mating urge that husband and wife were to have for each other. Therefore Adam and Eve enjoyed lovemaking. It was beautiful. This was designed by God to enrich the relationship between them for their entire married life.

But everything that God said was good in the first chapter of Genesis, Satan set about to pervert and destroy in chapter 3. One thing that the enemy wanted most of all was to tear down the normal sexual activities between husband and wife. What God gave to mankind for pleasure and procreation, Satan started to pervert. This included the normal sexual relations between man and woman.

When God created man and woman he created them heterosexual. This means different or against homosexuality. Sexual intercourse was to be done by different sexes, a male and a female, coming together so there would be procreation.

Man started to substitute what God had created beautiful for unnatural, unclean and perverted practices by joining themselves in a sexual way to people other than their spouses. This created bondages and they corrupted themselves by having a god in their life. They became slaves to the lust of the flesh. Rom. 1:24 tells us God's response where it says, *"Wherefore God also gave them up to uncleanness through the lusts of their own hearts, to dishonour their own bodies between themselves" KJV*

Man became so sinful and sexually perverted that God decided to destroy the earth with a flood. God gave instructions to Noah in regard to repopulating the earth. He was to bring two of each male and female into the ark. Intercourse was not to be homo meaning two of the same sex.

When God told Noah to bring the animals into the boat, He told him to bring them two by two, male and female, for reproduction as explained in Gen. 6:18-22. God didn't say to bring two males or two females of each. The earth would not have been repopulated after the flood if this had been the case. If they had been homo or of the same sex how could the reproduction of the races of man and of animals have taken place?

Generations passed. The earth was repopulated once again but we see that the deceiver was still active. We see the results of the work of the flesh that started to take place. Every form of corruption and whoredom was conceived and became rampant. We see the people of God slowly being seduced by the works of the deceiver and an outbreak of bodily pleasure and sensuality was growing and spreading.

Satan knew how to destroy God's people by enticing them to commit perversions amongst themselves. As we can see in Ex. 32:1-19, the people started to act wildly. They had already forgotten the miracles that they had seen in the desert.

The people were easily led astray when they didn't get what they wanted. They were a stiff-necked and self-willed people. No matter how many miracles God had done for them, they turned aside quickly from the goodness of God. In verse 25 of the same chapter, we see that after dancing they exposed themselves or made themselves naked to worship the golden calf. That was how wicked and rebellious they had become in such a short time.

James 1:15 give us an explanation of the workings of sin. *"Then when lust hath conceived, it bringeth forth sin: and sin, when it is finished, bringeth forth death." KJV*

Here are five keys that will help you to better understand how you become bound by sexual sin.

1. Temptation is an attack intended to lead one into sin. The deceiver will try to make you believe that anything goes. This is a bait to lure one into sin.

2. Lust means an excessive sexual desire or an intense appetite for sex. Satan will cause you to think that you have to have more and more to be satisfied.

3. Entice means to deceive or enchant. A person's will is being weakened by temptation and lust. They begin thinking of more deviant pleasures.

4. Wrongful imagination of perversion is sinful acts continually depicted before their eyes. The more they imagine the more real it becomes to them.

5. Sin means transgressing God's law, voluntarily breaking the rules or going astray. Once a person has deadened his conscience to the voice of God it is easy to entertain sin. I would like to give you and example.

A young man was sharing how he got involved in pornography. One day he found pornographic books under the couch. They belonged to his father who evidently was bound by this filth.

The devil plans his attacks and uses a strategy in every situation. A ruse was used to bring him into temptation and make him sin. He made it possible for this young man to be exposed to these books.

He said the first time he looked at them his curiosity was aroused. The images of sinful acts were always present in his mind. It didn't take much for this single young man to be ensnared. And it got worse. He started to search on the Internet for more erotic scenes, books, movies, and encouraging sexual talk for stimulation.

Those who engage in perversion or are entangled in wickedness are in darkness. Eph. 5:12, 13 tell us, *"And have no fellowship with the unfruitful works of darkness, but rather reprove them. For it is a shame even to speak of these things which are done of them in secret. But all things that are reproved are made manifest by the light: for whatsoever doth make manifest is light." KJV*

The enemy had a way of tracking the filth to keep him in slavery. Because of his father's bondage to pornography and perverse language, a door was open for his son to be lured into that filth. The son was now reaping what the father sowed.

You don't have to live under this bondage anymore. Bring this strong sexual drive under the control of the Holy Spirit. You need discipline as revealed in *1* Timothy 5:22 **"Flee also youthful lusts: but follow righteousness, faith, charity, peace, with them that call on the Lord out of a pure heart"**. KJV This will take some dedication to resist. Pray the following for the help of the Holy Spirit:

Father in the name of Jesus Christ I ask forgiveness for every involvement in sexual perversion. I break and renounce every spirits of Masturbation, Uncleanliness, Fornication, Adultery, Pornography, Lewdness, Perversion, Incest, Pedophile, Homosexuality, Lesbianism etc.... in the name of Jesus Christ. I renounce, break and loose myself from every satanic bondage, every evil influence that torments and defile me in Jesus name. I ask you Father to restore, heal and wash my mind, my soul and my body with the blood of Jesus Christ. I thank you Lord for setting me free. Amen

The Works of the Flesh

Using Gal. 5:19-21, I would like to explain the seventeen works of the flesh. *"Now the works of the flesh are manifest, which are these; Adultery, fornication, uncleanness, lasciviousness, Idolatry, witchcraft, hatred, variance, emulations, wrath, strife, seditions, heresies, Envyings, murders, drunkenness, revellings, and such like; of the which I tell you before, as I have also told you in the past, that they which do such things shall not inherit the kingdom of God." KJV*

1. Adultery: unlawful sexual intercourse between a married person and another not his spouse. The non-married also commits adultery. Unlawful sexual intercourse where at least one of the partner is married. They can have adulterous experiences in their thoughts by the Internet. Jesus said if a man even looks upon a woman he has committed adultery in his heart. Matt. 5:32; Matt. 5:19; and Matt. 19:9.

2. Fornication: voluntary sexual intercourse between married and unmarried people. Matt. 5:32; Matt. 19:9; I Cor. 7:2; 10:8; 1 Th. 4:3; and Rev. 9:21.

3. Uncleanness: morally impure, unchaste, obscene and all forms of sexual perversion as seen in Matt. 23:27; Rom. 1:24, 6:19; 2 Cor. 12:21; Eph. 4:19, 5:3; Col. 3:5, 7; 1 Th. 4:7; and 2 Peter 2:10.

4. Lasciviousness: tending to excite lustful desires, inward depravities, unchaste, wanton. Anything to promote sex, sin, lust and fleshly gratification.

Wicked and depraved lustful appetite. Mark 7:22; 2 Cor. 12:21; Gal. 5:19; 1 Peter 4:3; and Jude 4.

5. Idolatry: excessive devotion to or reverence for some person or thing. Idol worship of a person who has died or is alive. 1 Cor. 10:14; Gal. 5:20; Col. 3:5; 1 Peter 4:3; Eph. 5:5; and Col. 3:5.

6. Witchcraft: the practice of receiving supernatural power through evil spirits; casting spells and charms upon individuals by means of drugs and potions of various kinds. Isaiah 47:12-13; Rev. 9:21, 18:23; Rev. 21:8; and 22:15.

7. Hatred: strong dislike or ill will against somebody; holding grudges or being angry; aversion and hatred when offended. Eph. 2:15-16; James 4:4; and Gal. 5:20.

8. Variance: to quarrel or dispute; to bring disagreement and conflict; to encourage dissension by discord. Acts 15; 23:7-10.

9. Emulations: to rival or have jealousy; to covet the material possessions of others, their mate, to covet a higher level of education... Acts 13:45; 1 Cor. 3:3; 2 Cor. 12:20.

10. Wrath: intense anger, rage or fury especially for vengeance against somebody. Luke 4:28; Eph. 4:31; Col. 3:8; Heb. 11:27; and Rev. 12:12.

11. Strife: quarrels and divisions about words; civil strife and rage against one's authority; to bring division and conflict in family, marriage, siblings, etc. 2 Cor. 12:20; James 3:14, 16; Phil. 2:3; and Rom. 13:13.

12. Seditions: stirring up of rebellion against the government and religion; causing divisions

between others. Rom. 16:17; 1 Cor. 3:3; Luke 23:19-25; and Acts 24:5.

13. Heresies: any opinion opposed to the official church doctrine that cause a division; factions and dissensions. Acts 5:17, 15:5; and 1 Peter 2:1.

14. Envying: jealousy at the blessings of another; to covet or to turn green with jealousy; malice. Rom. 1:29; Rom. 13:13; Phil. 1:15; Titus 3:3; James 4:5; and 1 Peter 2:1.

15. Murders: premeditated killing of one human being by another; brutal; capable or intending to murder; hardness of heart. Matt. 15:19; Mark 7:21; 15:7; Luke 23:19-25; Rom. 1:29; Acts 9:1; Gal. 5:21; and Rev. 9:21.

16. Drunkenness: overcome by alcohol or being intoxicated and overcome by powerful emotion; to excite greatly and elate to a frenzy; a drug that intoxicates; a slave to alcohol. People will do things when they are drunk that they would never do when sober. A man's ability to reason and physical strength are all overcome by strong alcoholic drink. Gen. 9:21; Gen. 19:33; Luke 21:34; and Rom. 13:13.

17. Revellings: lascivious feastings with obscene music and other lustful activities with drunkenness. 1 Peter 4:3; and Rom. 13:13.

Oral Genital Sex

God gave laws on copulation in Lev. 15:16-18. Moral laws were given for our protection. God asks us to take as much care of our uncomely parts in our body as the honorable ones. The body was to function perfectly in unity.

Today men are taught to lust after their wife with deprave and debauched sexual practices. Because demons are insatiable, corruption will steadily increase in inordinate love.

We see movies, T.V. programs, books, songs and so on, propagate corrupt and unlawful practices. These entice Christians into deprave sexual activities forbidden by God.

I would like to show how one of these vile practices like oral sex could bring infestation of evil spirits and bring destruction. Here is an illustration.

When you drink fluids your body takes all the minerals and other nutrients to keep your body hydrated. Then it goes through your kidneys, washing away any impurities in your body. It then leaves your body as unclean water or urine. Urine is composed of uric acid, urea, ammonia and creatinine...

The same process happens with what you eat. The food you consume feeds your body all the vitamins and proteins to keep your blood healthy. Your digestive system breaks down into simpler elements the foods so it may be absorb in your bloodstream and is use for energy. After all this process has taken place, the digested food is evacuated into your intestine. Then it is discharged from your body as waste matter. We see this in Mark 7:19,

"Because it entereth not into his heart, but into the belly, and goeth out into the draught, purging all meats." In other words, the draught is the waste or feces.

When you are sick and you go to see a doctor to find out what is wrong, the first thing he will do is test your urine to see if there is any infection or blood. The same thing is done with the feces. The doctors will also test it to see if there is any blood in it or to find out what kind of sickness or disease you have. God knew about the uncleanliness of the waste that comes out of your body.

In oral genital sex some of those toxic substances are entering the mouth of the sexual partner. In fact, in Leviticus, God calls the seed of copulation unclean.
According to the Bible, a man and a woman must wash themselves and their clothes, bedding, etc. when soiled by the seed of copulation. If this seed of copulation or semen is considered unclean in an external way, we can assume that God never intended for it to go into the mouth. This is the reason He is against oral sex. Those who have AIDS or cold sores transfer these diseases by oral genital sex.

Some people are very fussy about what type of food goes into their mouth or are very disdainful of those who eat strange foods but don't think twice about putting someone's genitals in their mouth. This practice is dangerous and an abomination to God.

God understood the sexual drive He created in His creation. So for those who could not control their passions or who had a strong sexual appetite, He instructed that it was better to get married than to burn with lust. We see this in 1 Cor. 7:9 where it says, ***"But if they cannot contain, let them marry: for it is better to marry than to burn." KJV***

If you claim you are saved but have a yoke of lust that controls your thoughts, then you need deliverance. You cannot be free if there is a god in your life. You are still a slave and in bondage to sin.

Every time a person comes for deliverance and they are bound by the spirit of oral sex, the Holy Spirit will uncover or reveal this sin and the person is set free. We are what you would call heterosexual people and every sexual act that is done orally is abhorrence to God. When God ordained sex, copulation was to be done by penetration.

Many are saying that genital oral sex is foreplay to sexual intercourse. But when one is obsessed with it he is bound by an idol in his life. You know you are addicted to something when you either don't want to give it up or you can't. One man was sharing that he would never give up this practice for he loved it. When he revealed this to me I was troubled in my spirit. After he left, I started to pray asking God why I was troubled. This is what the Holy Spirit revealed. Those who didn't want to give up this lustful practice of oral sex were idol worshippers. Oral sex is a god in their life called self-worship. Their pleasure is more important to them than God. They enjoy oral sex and they would never give it up for anyone. It controls them. They cannot have normal sexual intercourse without being obsessed with this practice. Their lust is overpowering and it dominates them.

In Rom. 1:24 it is written, *"Wherefore God also gave them up to uncleanness through the lusts of their own hearts, to dishonour their own bodies between themselves." KJV*

God has not called us to a life of uncleanliness but rather to a life of holiness. Seek God. Choose to obey Him and know that His rules are for our good and protection. Treasure the things of God for as Matthew 6:31 says, *"For where your treasure is, there will your heart be also." KJV*

Incest

Another form of shame and abomination forbidden by God is the practice of incest. Incest is sexual intercourse and sexual perversion between family members too closely related for marriage, such as grandfathers, fathers, brothers, grandchildren, first cousins, mothers and sisters (Gen. 18:9). This also includes stepfathers, stepmothers, stepchildren, in-laws, etc. as explained in Lev. 18:6-18.

When man gets away from God, all kinds of fornication and immoral practices will be done. Because of ignorance of the scriptures parents cannot teach their children to protect themselves because of their own lack of knowledge. When children are growing up they learn by examples from their parents or elders. The sense of security that is provided by the parents is a reassurance and a necessity for maturing, healthy children.

When family members break trust through sexual abuse, a child's sense of security is broken. A door is opened for spirits of guilt, lust, lying, and hiding to come in.

When the abuser threatens them to silence, they innocently become an accomplice and a cooperator with the abuser. Their normal childish innocence is destroyed and they become nervous and insecure. They often can't sleep and are carrying a load that is too heavy for a child to carry.

I recall a young woman who was sharing how she was abused sexually at the age of ten by her older brother. She would awaken in the night frightened by a presence in her bedroom. She became very anxious, terrorized and paralyzed by fear until she had an emotional breakdown.

Her mother could not understand the cause of her sickness and brought her to numerous doctors. They could not find anything wrong with her. She grew up emotionally and physically unstable.

Later on in life when she got married, the nightly fears continued and she was unable to have a normal sexual relationship with her husband. After five years of marriage she was still reliving the traumatizing event that happened to her at the age of ten.

Much to the astonishment of her husband, the fear of her abuser returning during the night caused her to sometimes push a big dresser in front of her bedroom door. She was living in mental torment and guilt daily. This torment had arrested her development and she was acting like a little girl.

But after she came for help she was completely set free from this bondage and started to mature mentally.

Incest is one of the most hidden transgressions of our society. When one is being sexually abused, a door of silence is closed and the victim acts as if they are the guilty one. As a child they take on a responsibility they can't carry and their system breaks down under this abnormal pressure.

Others have testified that a door of lust had been opened and they were attracted to others who were bound by the same lust. Often the sexual abuse got worse.

We see that this is not new to our time or generation. Examples of this are seen early on in the Old Testament with the account of Lot and his two daughters in Gen. 20:11-36, and later, Amnon and Tamar in II Samuel 13:8, 11-14, and Herod and Herodias in Matt. 14:3-4. These examples show the shameful history and how they were cursed.

Parents must teach their children there is good touching and there is bad touching. Children must be taught that they have the right to say no to any contact that they feel is not right such as fondling, masturbation, oral sex, intercourse and anal sex. Many times the abuser will threaten the child and say that this is their secret and not to tell anyone.

Teach your children to never be afraid to come to you when there is something bothering them. Tell them you are there to protect and defend them and do not make the mistake of disbelieving them. Take the time to investigate so that there can be no doubt that it happened.

Since before the fall of man Satan's motive was to steal, kill and destroy. And the one he wants to destroy most of all is the innocent defenseless victim, your child.

But you can be set free from the enemy's attack. You can also have freedom from this terrible bondage of incest in the name of Jesus Christ through deliverance. God can free his people by whatever means He chooses. Jesus Christ is not limited. Ask Him and He will answer the way He sees fit and all He asks of us is to do our best. Praise God you can reclaim your self-esteem and be free. Alleluia!

Chapter 9

Ungodly Acquaintances

In 2 Cor. 6:13-18, the Bible tells us: *"**Don't be teamed with those who do not love the Lord, for what do the people of God have in common with the people of sin? How can light live with darkness? And what harmony can there be between Christ and the devil? How can a Christian be a partner with one who doesn't believe? And what union can there be between God's temple and idols? For you are God's temple, the home of the living God, and God has said of you, "I will live in them and walk among them, and I will be their God and they shall be my people." That is why the Lord has said, 'Leave them; separate yourselves from them; don't touch their filthy things, and I will welcome you, and be a Father to you, and you will be my sons and daughters'."** LB*

There was a Christian woman who had given up every worldly friend and carnal habit except for one long-time acquaintance. She was convinced that she could save her friend even though this friend repeatedly and emphatically said, "I will not become a Christian."

Every morning they would go for a walk and she (not the Holy Spirit) would minister to her friend. And each morning her friend would mock and laugh at her. In the beginning she held her ground, but gradually the spirit of doubt and unbelief began to sneak into her.

This friend was sucking the spiritual life right out of her. In tears, she called me and said, "I think I've lost my salvation." She admitted that she had not broken the ties with her unbelieving friend.

When she realized that only God could save her friend, she ended the relationship saying, "I can't see you until God changes your hardened heart. I have to go my own way."

She testified that after ending the association with her long-time friend, she felt as if a rope had been loosened from her chest and she found her close relationship with Jesus again.

The ungodly friend did not understand the desire of a born again believer to live and follow God daily. In 2 Cor. 6:17, the Bible plainly tells us to separate ourselves from anything unclean. I would like to give an example why we had to leave some friends.

When our children were teenagers, a man was trying to give advice to my husband on how to raise our children. He said, "Don't stop your children from drinking, give them alcohol, and give them beer. If you don't, they will go out and hide to drink."

I will always remember the answer my precious husband gave him. Roger, looking him straight in the eyes, very calmly said, "Children learn by example.

If, as a father, I sit at this table with a beer in my hand and try to tell my children not to drink because it isn't good for them, I would be a hypocrite.

If I want my children to follow a rule in my house then I have to be an example to them. It starts with me first. I have to be a role model to them. Oh, they might go and try to do things that are forbidden later on but there will always be a conviction on them for disobeying the rules we tried to teach them. I believe my example will follow them for the rest of their lives."

The man bowed his head and didn't answer for he himself was reaping what he had sown. He was having a terrible time with his young son who drank heavily and his other children were living in adultery.

They had no role model to look up to for the father was a heavy drinker himself. And yet he was trying to give us advice on how to raise our children.

To protect our children and family members we severed the relationship. We do not despise them but lift them up daily in prayer for their eyes to be opened to the tactics of the enemy.

So many children have ungodly parents as role models. This affects their lives and they become exactly, "like father like son" or "like mother like daughter". Living in such foolish self-indulgences will affect the mind and body of their offspring and they will also live in a permissive way. God will hold these parents accountable for the way they rear their children.

Newton (not his real name) was happy to have found the Lord but he didn't want to cut the ties with his unbelieving friends. He had one friend whose speech was filled with sexually degrading remarks toward women and his buddies laughed at this man's lewd speech. Although Newton didn't approve of this, he found his friend to be a reliable person who was always ready to lend a hand. When Newton shared his faith with his buddies they didn't want to "hear any of that crap".

Discouraged by their remarks, he began to doubt his faith and stopped reading the Word. He was becoming lukewarm, no longer on fire for the Lord. He was starting to doubt his own salvation.

After some time, he called me saying that he had committed the unpardonable sin of rejecting the Holy Spirit. He had lost his salvation.

The Holy Spirit revealed that satan had a legal hold on him through his pagan friends. He severed the relationship in love. He did not want them to think he was "holier than thou". He explained he was not trying to be better than they were but better than himself.

As a baby Christian, he was still struggling with the flesh and needed to protect himself from sin. And with prayer, his faith was restored.

Jesus Christ has commissioned us to tell the good news. According to 1Tim. 3:6-7, we learn it is not good to have a young convert teach the word of God for he is still a baby in the faith. He needs to mature spiritually. He lacks experience and has emotional baggage that needs to be broken. He still has struggles in the flesh.

Many born again Christians have taken on the responsibility of saving the whole world before being grounded in the word of God. They want to work for God instead of letting God work through them. Luke 14:28-32 tells us: *"But don't begin until you count the cost. * For who would begin construction of a building without first getting estimates and then checking to see if he has enough* (maturity, my quote) *money to pay the bills? Otherwise he might complete only the foundation before running out of funds. And then how everyone would laugh! " 'See that fellow there?' they would mock. 'He started that building and ran out of money before it is finished!' "Or what king would ever dream* *of going to war without first sitting down with his counselors and discussing whether his army of 10,000 is strong enough to defeat the 20,000 men who are marching against him? " If the decision is negative, then while the enemy troops are still far away, he will send a truce team to discuss terms of peace. So no one can become my disciples unless he first sits down and counts his blessings and then renounces them all for me." LB*

Chapter 10

The Curse of the Working Mother

Many working moms have come to me for help over the years. Many have related that after working on their careers all their lives, they felt they had accomplished much for others but had failed their families. Here is a mother's story.

"I realized after thirty-five years of trying to raise three children, getting them up very early in the morning, rushing them to the babysitter and then rushing off to work myself, that my day's work was never done.

I would arrive home and another rush would begin: getting supper, helping the children with their homework, rushing to piano lessons or hockey, ballet, baseball, football, horseback riding, gymnastics or whatever was on the program, baths and then bedtime.

By this time I would be so exhausted that I didn't have the energy to do anything else. The washing needed to be done, lunches needed to be made for the next day for the entire family, etc. I was worn out by the time I went to bed.

I didn't have time to give love to my children so I bought it by giving them material things. They were never satisfied, always wanting more. They became very selfish. I realized that they loved their baby-sitter more than they loved me since she was always there loving them, making crafts, playing with them and fussing over them when they were sick. They got all her attention.

When my children reach puberty I wanted to teach them rules to follow for their own protection. They looked me straight in the eye and said, 'We are not obliged to listen to you. You were never there for us.' My husband and I had given them everything they wanted and now they were used to having their own way. I had not taken the time to discipline or encourage them. And they rebelled against our authority and every word we said.

I continued to work, wondering how I could solve my problems. And there were many. Then they left for college and university. My husband and I worked hard to pay for their education. When they were through their school years they went to work in other cities."

She started to cry with heartbreaking sobs. When she was able to speak again, she revealed how lonely she was and how she wanted to hear their voices. She would phone them to find out how they were and though they were nice they were not warm and they were always in a hurry to end the conversation.

"I can feel the rejection from them. There is no place in their hearts for my husband or me. Now we are retired and we have all the time in the world for them. But it is too late. They don't want to have anything to do with us now.

You see when they were small, I was so busy rushing them that I didn't have the time to love or cherish my children. My selfish ambition was to build my career. It was more important to me and that was my priority. I gave them love by buying material things to appease my guilt.

I look back on my life and I have been rewarded with trophies and commendations but I am receiving none from my children. I have abandoned and rejected them and now it is too late to turn back the hands of time. The regrets I experience are heart wrenching.

During my career, I had many influential people around me, but those I want the most now are my children and they don't want me. When I want to see them I have to promise to buy them gifts. Only then will they come. I still have to buy their love, even to this day. They are cold and heartless and treat me the same way I treated them over their growing up years.

I have much wealth and I have accomplished much for others but nothing for my children. I am now looking back and would like to relive my life all over again. My career and wealth would not be my first priority. My own flesh and blood would come first. I am lonely, sick and have none who care about me. There are not enough tears to cry to heal my broken heart."

I have heard other testimonies like this repeated over and over again by those who have retired and come for help. They are tormented in their minds and have no peace. They never bonded with their children.

They have wealth and closets full of clothes. When they long to go on a trip, money is no problem. Whatever they want materially they can buy. Half their life is over only to discover that they have all the material abundance they yearn for but no love from those for whom they devoted their lifetime to acquire worldly goods. What a tragedy!

One young mother was sharing that she cried every morning when she left her young child at the babysitter's. When I asked her if she had to work this was her reply, "Not really. I work to buy what others have. If we don't have what everyone else has what will we look like?"

They wanted to compete with every "Jo Blow" on the block. Material possessions, which were usually bought on a plastic credit card, had more value in her eyes than giving maternal care and bonding with her baby.

To be able to look successful like every other "Tom", "Dick" and "Harry" who had boats, big television screens, brand new cars, the latest styles in clothing, traveled at will, etc. she was willing to have her heart broken daily by leaving her child in a daycare center or at a babysitter.

Deep down inside she didn't want to leave her little toddler but appearances were imposed on her by a society that delights in pride.

Some working moms have disclosed how they felt trapped by society's expectations. No matter how much they wanted to stay home and raise their own children the saying of, "What will the neighbors think if I don't have what they have or what will they say if I don't work?", keeps them working. People will say to them that they will not be fulfilled if they stay at home to be a mother and a wife.

The "if" and "what" of what others think is controlling their lives. So the mother is compelled to be in the working field to keep up with the "Jones".

However, as fast as the money comes in it goes out. They take part in every social event no matter how expensive it is. They have to keep up to the social status of looking rich in front of others. They don't want to be looked down upon by anyone.

Satan is controlling them by pride and lies. In Haggai 1:6 the Bible tells us that, *"You have sown much, but you have reaped little; you eat, but you do not have your fill; you clothe yourselves, but no one is warm; and he who earns wages has earned them to put them in a bag with holes in it." L.B.*

Their money is being sown to the whirlwind. They earn wages that do not meet their needs because of their extravagant lifestyle. They are always lacking, having no wisdom to save any money. Instead of budgeting their spending they buy whatever they want at will and travel at will.

They don't take the time to make their own meals. Quick fix suppers and restaurants are their cooks. They find out at the end of the month that no matter how big the salary of both husband and wife, the money spent is more than what they brought in.

Because of the expectations of others, their whole life is being manipulated and dictated by the "Jones" and the "Smiths". They never have enough. The curse of destitution is always following them.

These are some examples of hurting people who want out but are controlled by a worldly society. Satan has a stronghold over their money and he wants to make sure that they lack wisdom to save it.

The role of being a mother and a wife has been so downgraded by the feminist movement. Mothers are afraid to stay home for fear of being laughed at. The feminist groups say the woman has been liberated. They say she's made for greater things than raising children; that she can do anything that a man can do.

But what they do not say is that the working mother has more work than she bargained for. Her duties never end. After working all day and though she comes home at night mentally and physically tired, she still has a number of tasks awaiting her. She has to be a superhuman mom to be able to accomplish all that is required of her. It gradually depletes her physical and emotional resources and she pays a great price for these Herculean efforts.

Some mothers have stated that because of separation, divorce or the death of their husband they have to work, being the only breadwinner. The worry of not having enough money to provide for their offspring is putting stress and pressure on them.

They cannot afford to be sick for that means the loss of a day's wage for those who are paid by the day. No matter how tired they are, they have to pull themselves out of bed every morning. They have to forget about their personal needs and out of necessity are forced to comply with a rigid schedule. Destitution and poverty seems to be their lot.

Some are always lacking. Bad luck seems to follow them. Others are always living on the poverty line. Some, because of sickness, are unable to work while others always seem to be losing their jobs. The thief is always at their back. Destitution follows them everywhere.

Because of insufficient funds to pay for the necessities of life, mothers and daughters are obliged to be in the workplace. Some work because it's a choice they voluntarily make and they enjoy working. Others work out of sense of competition for materialistic gain. For many it's an obligation to provide for great needs.

Because of the working mother, children have become a commodity to lug around like baggage. Children feel neglected and abandoned and the result is troubled and delinquent children.   In Eph. 6:4 the scriptures reveal: *"And ye fathers, provoke not your children to wrath: but bring them up in the nurture and admonition of the Lord." KJV* With mothers working, there is no longer the supervision and guidance to protect and guide the footsteps of the children.   They have become self-willed and spoiled with hardened hearts. They've missed out on the daily love that only a mother can give.

It was not meant to be this way.   God provided a male and a female to be partners in raising their children. He gave each a specific role.   Adam was to be the worker, the provider.   Eve was to be his helpmeet, to bear the children and to care for them.

When Adam sinned, a curse came upon the earth and he lost his full dominion over the animals, the herbs, the vegetation, the fruits and the soil.   He and Eve were to have lived forever in abundance but after the curse, they had to toil for their livelihood.

Because of this judgment, we are today still reaping the consequences of all the numerous curses of hardship that cause poverty, lack, want and destitution.

When God said in Gen. 1:28 to be fruitful, this meant to be fertile.   If you look in the Webster's dictionary, fertile means to produce abundantly, to be rich in resource and invention.   This means that we were not to live in poverty.   There was to be sufficient abundance to supply all of our needs.

God blessed us with great intelligence.   But because of the bondage of sin we are not able to use, to the greatest capacity, all the intelligence with which God created us.

If you recognize your greed or your pride, put a stop to it right now and ask God's forgiveness. Renounce the "what will others say or what will they think" attitude and start living your own life. Don't be controlled anymore by the opinions or the expectations of others. It takes a strong backbone not to comply with the viewpoints of all your neighbors and family.

Don't be taken in by Satan's lies that you cannot be fulfilled as a mother and as a wife. The devil's work is to steal your wisdom, your peace, your children and your money. In John 10:10 we read, ***"The thief cometh not, but for to steal, and to kill, and to destroy: I am come to that they might have life, and that they might have it more abundantly." KJV***

Ask yourself, "Why am I working? Is it out of necessity or am I being controlled by a spirit of greed, insecurity, dissatisfaction or a lack of contentment?" Bring every one of these curses to the cross. And God will provide for your means if you depend on Him for your provision.

Jesus has given us the authority in His Name to claim back our inheritance to be able to live in abundance. Therefore, moms can stay home and take care of their treasures. They can bond with their offspring and the children will be nurtured and loved. You can pray this prayer:

"Father in the name of Jesus Christ I break every curse of destitution, poverty and debt that was handed down to us by my family and my forefathers. I revoke every one of those curses over us and our offspring and I break every demonic hold on us right now in Jesus' Name. Satan, I command you to take your hands off our finances. Father, I ask for wisdom to stretch those dollar bills and to restore what was stolen from us (John 10:10). By the authority of Jesus Christ I ask to be redeemed from this curse of debt. I ask your Holy Spirit to send forward your ministering angels (Heb. 1:14) to open the doors that were closed and to restore what was stolen from me and my family. Lord, I ask for special blessings to be released in our lives that I will be able to stay home and raise our children. Lord, I thank you for a financial breakthrough and I give you all the glory in the precious Name of Jesus."

Chapter 11

The Spirit of Anger

One of the tactics the enemy will use in controlling your character is anger. If a person has a spirit of anger or violence, you will see by their actions that something is making them react or scream the way they do. Evil impostors tyrannize them. They are like a puppet in the hands of Satan. They have no self-restraint. A spirit of anger and violence is ruling their life. Even if they are born again Christians they are confronted daily with the flesh as stated in Rom. 6:12.

They need to break the enemy's control over their sinful desires. Paul said through deliverance they could be set free. They have the power to break the cycle of losing control of their temper, by breaking and renouncing the curse of anger and violence, in the name of Jesus.

Many kinds of anger will be revealed through the gift of discerning of spirits. One man was raised in a family where physical abuse was the rule. The spirits of violent anger and rage were transferred down to him. The only way he knew how to react when he was mad was to slap and punch. His wife and children were in great turmoil from these sudden bursts of rage. The Holy Spirit exposed the thief in his life and he was finally set free.

Another person was so angry at the abuse and harsh authority in her home that she was defiant and resistant to every rule of her parents. The spirit of rebelliousness and vicious anger got her into many hardships. After deliverance, she was finally set free of the enemy who had control of her character and her life for so long.

Another who came for deliverance was bound by anger. He told me how God had protected him from killing his wife who was always accusing him. He said, "When she started to blame me, I denied every charge." This went on for a few years. When she would start criticizing him, he would get very upset and anger would start to rise inside of him. A door was opened for the enemy to take control. He said he was a very gentle person, normally, but being under this continuous battering of accusation he started to change. He said, "A spirit of blue anger took control of me. I had to leave my wife for if I had stayed with her I would have killed her."

During the deliverance session, the Holy Spirit uncovered the enemy's tactic to keep this family in bondage. He was set free and learned how to resist the enemy. The marriage was restored.

Another came for deliverance because she was losing control. When something happened that upset her, she would start to break or throw every object in front of her. She would throw tantrums and what came out of her mouth was destructive. She had a time bomb inside of her ready to explode. She had a spirit of destructive anger. She was afraid of what she could do while under this influence. A thief was in control.

I asked her if she had always been like this and this is what she answered. "It started when a co-worker, who wanted my position, started a rumor that I was stealing in my workplace. I was hurt and enraged for I knew it was not true. I lost my job because of it. I was devastated. I became uncontrollable. Anger kept festering. I got so furious and angry because of this injustice. Even now when this spirit takes control of my mind, I lose it. I am afraid of my next move."

Here we see a door was opened for a spirit of uncontrollable anger to possess her. Through deliverance, her eyes were opened to see the bondage she was in and she was gloriously set free. She was able to forgive.

When the enemy uses another person to get at you, he does not care how much destruction he dishes out on you. All he wants is for his spirits to have a house to live in so he can control your life.

Reclaim the ground that Satan has stolen from you! You do not have to live like a slave anymore. Become a conqueror, not a defeated one. The scriptures tell us in Rom. 7:19-20 that, *"When I want to do good, I don't; and when I try not to do wrong, I do it anyway. Now if I am doing what I don't want to, it is plain where the trouble is: sin still has me in its evil grasp". LB*

When you draw near to God and ask to be set free of the spirits that are oppressing or tormenting you, you should come clothed in humility, having genuine repentance in your hearts. You may feel compelled to lie to conceal the sin present in your life but this is a time to be truthful. When the Holy Spirit reveals areas of bondage, you should not be afraid to accept what is discerned.

Chapter 12

The Spirits of Criticism and Jealousy

A Christian woman had come seeking information on the gift of discerning of spirits. As I was explaining the gift she interrupted me saying, "You have pierced ears! Did you know that is a sin? You shouldn't have pierced your ears because you need to be an example of Christianity." When she finished rebuking me she then asked, "Do you mind if I have a cigarette? I haven't kicked the habit yet."

I was stunned into silence! The following verse came to mind from Matt. 7:3-5, *"And why worry about a speck in the eye of a brother when you have a board in your own? Should you say 'Friend, let me help you get that speck out of your eye,' when you can't even see because of the board in your own? Hypocrite! First get rid of the board. Then you can see to help your brother." LB*

Further on into our conversation, she revealed how she had lost a child in a car accident and how she couldn't forgive the Lord for taking her child. She felt bitter and angry with God and yet she was in the habit of telling others how to live for Christ.

What a shameful and profane example of Christianity. While reprimanding others for the insignificant specks in their eyes, she had overlooked the log in her own eyes.

Satan is a usurper of the freedom you can have in your life. When the deceiver is given a foothold he becomes a tyrant who leads his victims around and around like a bear with a ring in its nose, having no will of their own. But you don't have to live this way. You can be set free with the powerful name of Jesus.

Once Satan is exposed, he will no longer have any legal ground in which to operate. Praise the name of Jesus, our wonderful Savior for the victory you can have in His precious Name.

Another area where evil spirits will transfer their character into a person is through jealousy. The one who is jealous is controlling, dominating and acts very suspicious. Their irrational mind will see or imagine things that are not real.

They will fabricate scenarios that become so real, the accusing one will actually believe they really happened. Bondage and pressure will be placed on their spouse or their relationships. Jealousy will cause division, strife and lack of trust in the other partner. The spirit of false accusation and condemnation will become uncontrollable.

Any visitor or individual to whom the partner talks will become a suspected threat. As a result, they are held on a tight leash with no freedom to be themselves. In Proverbs 6:34 we see, *"jealousy is the rage of a man"* and in Song of Solomon 8:6, *"jealousy is cruel as the grave."*

If a person is jealous without a reason to be jealous, then look for an evil spirit that is controlling and obsessing the imagination of that person.

Here are some areas where there are open doors for a spirit of jealousy to enter.

When a parent favors one child over another it opens a door for the spirit of jealousy, envy and competition. This will cause division between the siblings that will affect them throughout their lifetime.

If trust between a married couple has been broken because of adultery, then there is an open ground for a spirit of jealousy to develop.

I will give you an example. One night I was going to a meeting with a couple. I arrived at their home a little earlier than suggested, as I didn't want them to have to wait for me. Upon entering the house the wife greeted me warmly while her husband, who was seated at the far end of the table, got up to offer me a chair.

His wife took the chair that he was offering, banged it on the floor and preceded to tell me where to sit. I was ill at ease for I knew this woman was terribly jealous. The air was so thick that I could have cut it with a knife. She was glaring at him as if he had committed a crime. This poor husband bowed his head not even daring to say another word.

I asked his wife a question and while she was answering she never looked at me. She was glaring at her husband to see if he was to make eye contact with me. He looked so miserable, shifting on his chair as if he was sitting on hot coals.

I glanced sideways at her. Her eyes were suspicious and she was very distrustful. Even her face reflected the possession. I could literally see Satan controlling her personality.

In this example we see how jealousy can change even the outward appearance of a person. We also see the character of the person changing before our eyes as the spirits change them from rational to irrational.

Their two children, about nine and twelve years old, were watching the whole scenario. Sadly, they were witnesses to this sick kind of display daily. Here was another breeding ground for the same evil spirit of jealousy to continue the identical bondage in their lives. They were very vulnerable.

Children learn from what they see. They are like sponges. They soak up everything. These children were picking up, from their mother, the same spirit of jealousy and control.

This man was literally oppressed and destroyed mentally, had no self-esteem, and was unable to defend himself because he had a weak mind. She dominated his every move for she ruled the coop through the spirits of jealousy that were controlling her.

Parents are role models. Children imitate them. As a parent, you will pass down to your children either a blessing or a curse by your example.

Renounce addictive habits and break the shackles of iniquity with which Satan has bound you. You can say no to obsessive lifestyles and temptations! From James 4:7 we learn to, ***"Submit yourselves therefore to God. Resist the devil, and he will flee from you." KJV***

In the name of Jesus you can be set free by breaking every spirit of jealousy that is coming against your thoughts, your mind, your will and your emotions as soon as they are presented to you.

You can also break the curse of jealousy that came down to you through your bloodline and if you want freedom pray the following prayer:

Heavenly Father I bow in praise and worship before you. You said if I humble myself before you, you will open doors that otherwise would be closed. I renounce, break and command every spirits of jealousy, suspiciousness, distrust etc to leave me now in the name of Jesus. I reclaim the ground that satan has stolen from me. Lord I believe and I receive deliverance right now from these tormenting spirits that have harassed me for so long. In the name of Jesus Christ I believe and I receive freedom in my mind. Let your Holy Spirit encamp around my mind, my thoughts, my will and my emotion and cover me with your blood. And Lord how I thank you for being Our God, Our Savior and Our Guide. I ask you to protect me and show me the way in Jesus' name. Amen

Chapter 13

The Spirit of Offense

In this chapter, I will bring to light the spirit of offense and how to be delivered of it. In Webster's Dictionary an offense means: to create anger, or to hurt one's feelings, to insult someone. In Greek it means to cast a snare before someone to destroy him.

When someone is a baby in the faith and just beginning to grow, the fleshly part of "me, myself and I" goes into action when they are hurt. Self-pity comes to the surface when one is offended. They think they are not the guilty one, wondering what caused the injustice. One word said in anger or in judgment will prick their sensitivity to the core. They will want to find an audience to tell others how they have been hurt or insulted, wanting them to sympathize with their sense of affront or insult.

When a person is offended they become overly sensitive, watching every word and every gesture that might mean something. Then they go home and start to build a mountain out of misplaced words. They want the one who offended them to pay a price for what they have said. They become angry and resentful and will do anything not to meet that person again.

How far will one go to avenge personal injury? When a person is offended, the first thing that comes to mind is revenge. Some try to ease the pain by spending a fortune in lawyer fees. Proverbs 18:19 says, *"A brother offended is harder to be won than a strong city: and their contentions are like the bars of a castle."* **KJV**

In the workplace an offense will often cause strife, division and bad blood between co/workers. Someone in authority will degrade or harm persons because of their appearance, their personality or their social standing, etc. Great harm is done when one indiscriminately voices their critical opinions. The individual who has suffered the injury will be devastated, resentful, and carry anger inside.

When an offense is committed in a home, a school, a workplace or in a church, the only way to get rid of the insult or hurt is to forgive the one who offended you. It will take time and practice to overcome. But you will find that when you forgive, it releases your mind of all the tension, revenge, anxiety and unforgiveness that eats at your soul and steals your serenity. Then and only then will you have peace.

When an offense is committed and it causes division, Satan is happy since there is often a wall of silence. This silence keeps people in bondage and stunts their spiritual growth. Family members refuse to speak to one another for years on end.

If you have an offense against a family member, make amends while that person is still alive. You will not have serenity. Many tears are shed because of regret. You will be the one who will suffer.

We often see a spirit of offense in marriage breakdowns. When a divorce takes place in a family, a vendetta is often carried on for years toward the one who has done wrong, even turning the children against the former spouse out of anger and revenge. It often lasts for years.

A young woman came to see me for deliverance. She was very sick, depressed and on medication to ease her mental torment. As we were praying, the Holy Spirit unveiled a "spirit of hate". I asked her what it meant. She started to explain to me what had happened to her when she was a young child in school. While reading her literature she made a mistake in pronunciation. Her teacher laughed at her. She was so embarrassed and humiliated that it affected her self-esteem and she had carried bitterness and revenge in her soul for all these years. Because of unforgiveness and a spirit of offense, she was the one who still paid for what had happened fifteen years ago. She was so aggravated that she used all her energy to keep herself in turmoil. She suffered physically and was in mental torment daily. A lifetime of sorrow and pain had been hers because of these careless words.

In Matt. 18:34-35, Jesus said that if we fail to forgive we would be delivered to tormentors. This is what happened to this young woman. The destroyer had used a person in authority to destroy her. He had a good laugh at her misery. What a deceiver and a destroyer of happiness! After so many years of bondage, she was finally set free through deliverance in the precious name of our Lord Jesus. She is now living in victory.

One factor that will hinder a person from making peace is "pride". I've heard people say, "Chicken will have teeth before I forgive." This means never. If you don't forgive, then a door is open for evil spirits to slowly destroy you. Every day you are going to be tested by the opposing forces of darkness and your faith will be tried. You have a choice. Are you going to hold resentment or are you going to forgive and pray for the one who offended you? If you forgive you will be the winner and your mind will not be in continuous turmoil, but will be at peace. You will not always live in guilt but in peace. You will not always be planning revenge but when you forgive, those who have treated you wrongfully will be put to shame (see Rom. 12:20-21).

Satan has the right to go where doors have been opened by sin. When you fail to forgive you can expect a visit from the thief who is only too ready to steal, kill and destroy (see John 10:10).

Every action, every thought, every word that is lived contrary to the law will have consequences on your health and your bloodline. But we can have victory in Jesus. Thank God He gave His only Son, Jesus Christ, who died on the cross and shed His blood for the forgiveness of our sins. Through Him you can have peace and victory.

I will give you an example of the process I went through to overcome this weakness in my flesh. One person I knew was furious at me for leaving the religion I was raised in. He would attack me with condemnation and criticism every time I came face to face with him. I was hurt because of this injustice.

In the beginning I would defend my actions. But it seemed that the more I tried, the worse it got. So I quit trying. But I was enraged inside. When I would leave his place, a battle would take place in my mind and I would replay the conversation over and over, telling him to mind his own business. My faith was between God and myself and he was not going to dictate my beliefs. I fell into judgment every time I saw him. Then I would ask forgiveness of my Savior for my judgmental attitude. It was a vicious cycle and I got tired of it all.

One day in desperation I cried, "God help! What am I supposed to learn from all this." I had finally bent my knee. I was letting go of this mental battle. The reply came that I was offended. I wondered how to let it go.

The Holy Spirit revealed that when this individual came to mind or when I was talking to him, I was to send back love and forgive him no matter what he said. I started to pray for him. It was not easy to begin with but I found peace. According to 2 Cor: 2:10,11 *" When you forgive anyone, I do too. And whatever I have forgiven (to the extent that this affected me too) has been by Christ's authority, and for your good. A further reason for forgiveness is to keep from being outsmarted by Satan; for we know what he is trying to do.* And Matt. 6:12 says *"and forgive us our sins, just as we have forgiven those who have sinned against us." LB*

Just when I thought I had victory, another obstacle was sent my way to harass me. I thought the first battle was hard but this next one was worse.

A lady I knew started to spread evil slander about me. She didn't know me personally or the work I was doing in this ministry. This woman had a subtle way of manipulating people. She would twist the truth to her advantage and always get away with it. Stories she said about me were untrue and unfounded.

As a Christian, I could not seek revenge however, I was seeking revenge in my thoughts. After six weeks of turmoil, anger and rage, I pleaded with God to show me what to do.

The answer that came was two-fold: first to forgive her. Do you think I wanted to forgive her? Not for the life of me. But if I wanted to find peace in my soul I had to do it. I started to pray for her. At first it was only with my words and not with my heart. But gradually, as I poured blessing on her, the pressure started to lift off me and I found peace.

The battle was won for me when I forgave. Through this process I learned that if I didn't forgive I was not going to be set free.

Forgiveness not only releases mental torment, resentment, bitterness and hate but it is a way of life. When you forgive you impart an act of mercy on those who have wounded you.

In James 5:16 we are to, *"Confess your faults one to another, and pray one for another, that ye may be healed. The effectual fervent prayer of a righteous man availeth much." KJV*

The only way God forgives your transgression is when you forgive or have mercy on others. The principle of forgiveness was given when our Lord gave us the pattern for prayer in these verses in Mark 11:25-26 where it says, *"And whenever you stand praying, if you have anything against anyone, forgive him and let it drop (leave it, let it go), in order that your Father Who is in heaven may also forgive you your (own) failings and shortcomings and let them drop. But if you do not forgive, neither will your Father in heaven forgive your failings and shortcomings." AMP*

In Matt. 5:23-24 we also see, *"So if you are standing before the altar in the Temple, offering a sacrifice to God, and suddenly remember that a friend has something against you, leave your sacrifice there beside the altar and go and apologize and be reconciled to him, and then come and offer your sacrifice to God. Come to terms quickly with your enemy before it is too late and he drags you into court and you are thrown into a debtor's cell." LB* As you can see, there are consequences when you hold resentment and bitterness against someone. When you give a foothold to the enemy, he has an open door to bring torment of various forms and which, in turn, will cause all kinds of sickness.

Ps. 91:4 explains that when we stay under God's feathers and wings (which is a figure of speech for protection and care), Satan will not be able to use wickedness to ensnare us.

I had strayed from God's protection and a door was opened for the enemy to torment me with bitterness, resentment and harassment. I now know to forgive my enemies immediately in order to stay under God's protection.

I overcame the habit of going through the fire every time I was offended. The negative mind control that kept me captive with resentment and unforgiveness against the one who offended me seemed to dissolve when I learned to forgive. I was able to express the love of Jesus that was locked inside of me.

It was the most painful experience I had to go through at the time. Do you think my battle was over? No. Does one ever get used to evil slander? I don't believe anyone ever gets used to this powerful form of destruction. But I do believe you can learn not to be devastated when it happens.

Then when I learned to send love instead of hate and forgiveness instead of resentment, that was the second part of the Godly answer. I was the one who was blessed. I had peace in my heart.

Now when a spirit of offense comes my way, I might dwell on it for a moment or two but when I realize what the enemy is trying to do, I start praying and breaking the destructive forces of evil slander that is being sent my way. When the thief has been bound and is unable to function, this spirit of evil slander will not oppress you anymore. I put a stop to it by praying this prayer against the evil slander.

"Father, in the name of Jesus I break and bind every negative force, gossip and evil slander that is coming against me in the name of Jesus. I cover my thoughts, my mind, my will and my emotions with the blood of Jesus Christ. I pour showers of blessing on the one who is doing the damage. Lord I put a spirit of conviction upon (name the person) so they will become ashamed of what they have said about me. I break every power of evil slander that is over, around and under them and I break every spirit of strife, division and mental torment it will cause me who has been damaged because of evil slander in Jesus' Name. I thank you Father and I send your Holy Spirit to heal every wound in Jesus' Name. Amen."

Chapter 14

The Spirit of Fear

Another area where Satan can control your character is through fear. Satan is a liar and a murderer. Spirits of fear torment, harass and ravage one's life. They deceive God's people by putting paralyzing and terrorizing fear into their minds. This is in direct opposition to faith in God.

Fear sometimes puts a person in such agony that it controls his/hers every thought. Fear is not of God. In 2 Tim. 1:7 we see, ***"For God has not given us a spirit of fear, but of power, and of love and of a sound mind." KJV***

In the Garden of Eden when God came in the evening and called to Adam saying, "Where are you?" and Adam replied, "I am hiding." God asked him why he was hiding. And in Gen. 3:10, Adam replied, "I was afraid." The spirit of fear was revealed.

Now you may ask, "How did the spirit come in since Adam was not born with a spirit of fear?" The answer is simple. It was caused through sin. Adam's disobedience brought an evil spirit of fear and shame. He was bound. Satan had tricked him with his lies.

Today, when you stray from God, Satan uses this same method of introducing fear. These oppressors keep people in bondage. Satan is a thief who steals peace from the hearts of those bound by fear.

Jesus died on the cross to destroy the works of the devil. In 1 John 3:8 we read, ***"But if you keep on*** *sinning, it shows that you belong to Satan, who since he first began to sin has kept steadily at it. But the Son of God came to destroy these works of the devil." LB*

Paralyzing fear often stops people from defending themselves. One helpless victim of fear was being told by demons that if she went through deliverance they would attack her parents, her children and her husband. She believed this lie of the devil and cancelled her session for deliverance. She was under such bondage and oppression that she couldn't even trust God to set her free.

I told her that these were demonic lies and that she could be set free in the name of Jesus Christ. After much prayer she finally came for deliverance and was gloriously set free.

Upon learning of the tactics that Satan had used to keep her deceived and in bondage for so many unhappy years, she was angry. She is now living a victorious Christian life. Praise the Lord! Scriptures tell us in John 8:36 that, *"He that believeth on the Son hath everlasting life: and he that believeth not the Son shall not see life; but the wrath of God abideth on him." KJV*

Another example of how Satan kept someone captive with his lies involved a middle-aged woman who came to be set free of fear. She had been a Christian her entire life, was highly educated and very intelligent.

She came at the appointed time and as she entered my house she began to tremble excessively. She was overcome with fear, reacting and crying like a frightened child. She choked, "I feel like I am going to be sick," and finally chose to leave.

Twice she made an appointment; twice she cancelled. She had lived with this overwhelming fear all her life and it had become her companion.

It took her quite some time and a lot of prayer before she mastered the fear and came to be delivered of the spirits of fear, anxiety, timidity, panic, terrorizing and paralyzing fear, worry, dread, etc.

]Being a Christian does not stop Satan from harassing you and trying to bring you down. He uses fear and lies to keep you from a victorious life in Jesus. He weakens our Christian testimony, dimming the light of Christ within us and robbing us of our light.

In Matt. 5:13-16 it says, *"Ye are the salt of the earth: but if the salt has lost his savour, wherewith shall it be salted? it is thenceforth good for nothing, but to be cast out, and to be trodden under foot of men. Ye are the light of the world. A city that is set on an hill cannot be hid. Neither do men light a candle, and put it under a bushel, but on a candlestick; and it giveth light unto all that are in the house. Let your light so shine before men, that they may see your good works and glorify your Father which is in heaven."* **KJV**

The spirits of fear will try to steal your peace. Many are afraid to speak up when a problem arises for fear of being humiliated or embarrassed. Others who are wounded will mask their true feelings by putting on a façade that is phony. The hurt will make one bitter and he will blame others for his weakness – the fear of speaking up.

The next testimony is how Rosa was kept in bondage because of fear:

Rosa's Story

When I was small my neighbor looked after me most of the time when my mother became ill. My aunt and uncle took me at about six months of age and cared for me. It was a happy time and I loved them.

I came back to live with my family after my mother's health improved. My father was raised in a family whose father was controlling. He never could prove himself so he became an alcoholic.

My mother carried a baggage of resentment and bitterness. She was a very unhappy woman. Mom and Dad had been married only three years when they separated. There was constant verbal abuse and strife.

As children we were terrified and always dreading the next fight. The two most important people in our lives were born with so much baggage they didn't know how to cope with us.

After their separation, it was very hard to see them going through the hard times and being so miserable. Mom was counted on to take over the family matters. She worked very hard as a seamstress and also kept a few thousand hens to make enough money to support and care for us. She was withdrawn and preoccupied with her own sorrow, resentment and disappointments.

Growing up I felt so empty and insecure. Living in this environment I became very tense, anxious and overactive because of nervousness. I was always looking for approval from my mom. I seemed to be quite a handful for she often said I should have been a boy. I felt very rejected by her for she never showed any love. She never bonded with me. I learned to mask my true feelings in many ways.

We were reared in a strict home. Dad came to visit about once a week. We looked forward to seeing him. He would often bring us treats and sometimes things he had made. Many times he had been drinking when he came and that would start a fight.

We didn't have many visitors except for an aunt and uncle on my mom's side and the minister about once a year.

Mom became more of a recluse as time went on and we learned it was not good to have her angry with us. She didn't usually hit us but her way of disciplining us was through mental abuse.

When we disobeyed, her way of chastising us was not speak to us until we made known to her how sorry we were. This could last for 2 or 3 weeks. When she started to speak again, she would let us know that we didn't meet her standards and probably never would. This was mainly due to Dad's genetic influence.

I was never encouraged and I denied my own needs and true feelings. I grew up quickly and never had the freedom of being a child. I was acting like a woman before my time.

At about nine years of age I did most of the shopping. I had a lot of responsibility. Money was given to me and I had to budget it. I learned at a very young age to be super responsible.

Dad had a major stroke and Mom agreed with the doctors to have him live with us for a while. That was a big mistake. No one realized the pressure we, the children, were under as a result of the dysfunctional home we lived in daily. We were always on edge, never knowing when a fight would begin. My stomach was always in turmoil. I was emotionally drained all the time.

I became a pacifier for I was always trying to bring peace. Because of being so fearful and not wanting to be the cause of the next arguments I retreated into myself to find security.

As the daughter of an alcoholic, I tried to become invisible but I felt split between them both for I loved them dearly. I wanted to be loyal and devoted to both of them even if they didn't deserve such loyalty. I became very uneasy around other people, especially authority figures,.

About six months later my dad's health improved physically but things began deteriorating in the home. It was a battleground with its own little territories (my mom didn't want to be in the same room as my dad since he was drinking again).

One night they had a major fight. My father threatened to kill us all with a shotgun. I was terrorized with fear. I prayed for God to protect and keep us safe and He did.

I had very few friends. My way of dealing with being in a pressure cooker all the time was to spend a lot of time with my pets, drawing and bird watching.

My nerves were affected and I was on medication for a while. Being raised in a home where there was only negativity stole my peace and I suffered greatly for many years. I had nightmares for a long time.

My mother had tried to instill in us a hate for men because of her own unhappiness. It didn't work.

I became a Christian and not long after I met my wonderful husband. My mother didn't come to my wedding for she didn't approved. She didn't trust any man and hated them with a passion.

My marriage gift from her was the curse, "You will never be happy." She was a very stubborn woman. When she decreed a law it was followed religiously. After she passed away, we moved to another country.

When my children were growing up I wanted to give them what I didn't have. Because I was victimized, I had an overdeveloped sense of responsibility. When I took a stand with my children when they needed to be reprimanded I felt guilty all the time. I was very hard on myself.

When we needed money I felt it was my fault if there was a lack of funds. I had to find myself a job, even if I was ill. That is how fear had warped my mind.

In this new country, I met a woman with the gift of discerning of spirits and I had intensive deliverance. I was set free of many bondages of my forefather's sin. I reclaimed the ground satan had stolen from me.

These are some of the thieves I was delivered of: fear of violence, rejection from the womb, fear of happiness, fear of sickness, fear of mental abuse, fear of men, insecurity, no self worth, introversion, fear of people, hate to be judged, anorexia, nervousness, fear of expressing myself, hating to be condemned, fear of being rejected, fear of being abandoned, depression, loss of joy, etc.

Every day is a new day and I am learning how to overcome the bondage that kept me prisoner all these years. I praise God daily for my freedom.

If my father and my mother had known about the gift of discerning of spirits, Satan would not have been able to bring destruction on our family life.

I have three children and I have broken the curse of the forefathers on them. I praise God for His wisdom, and would like to tell others who are going through the same family turmoil that there is hope. We have the power to break the bondage that is oppressing us today. In the precious name of our Lord Jesus Christ, we have the freedom to claim back our inheritance that was stolen from us.

Chapter 15

In Jesus' Name

In His earthly ministry, Jesus spent much time teaching and explaining what evil spirits will do to the character or personality of a person.

One of the first things we see is a battle taking place between two kingdoms – the kingdom of God and the kingdom of Satan.

From the beginning, God's will was never for His children to subsist in poverty, be sinful and corrupt, or live in crime. Nor were we to be diseased, have infirmity, live in sin, have a filthy lifestyle, be unhappy in marriage or work. This was not His plan for us. But because Satan came along enticing man to sin and warping what God had ordained for us from the beginning, God wanted to show you there is a way out.

In His Word, God promised that each believer could have the power of attorney (in Jesus name) to destroy the works of the deceiver. He (Jesus) became the Mediator between God and men as seen in John 14:6 and 1 Tim. 2:5 to bring reconciliation.

The apostles had faith to heal and set the captives free when they used the name of our great Redeemer in Luke 10:17 *"And the seventy returned again with joy, saying, Lord, even the devils are subject unto us through thy name."* KJV. They gave all the glory back to our Lord Jesus Christ for when they spoke His precious name the captives were set free. This power was not only for the disciples or the early church but it is also for believers today.

In John 14:12-14, Jesus delegated his authority to the believers for healing, preaching, worship, praise and intercessory prayer.

If trials and testing have caused you to harden your heart, you have a Savior to whom you can turn to be delivered and set free. You can be free from guilt and condemnation by confessing, repenting and asking forgiveness.

You have the authority, in His Name, to bind the power of darkness and free yourselves from the oppression of the enemy. You don't have to live in mental torment for the rest of your pilgrim journey (Heb. 11:13) here on earth. You can be set free in the powerful name of our Savior, Jesus Christ.

When Jesus delegated His authority to the believer the condition was for one to believe in Him. Each born again believer can be endued with power to do the work of Jesus. When he died, he left us with another comforter as revealed in John 14:16-17. He didn't leave us a powerless comforter. To His rightful successors He gave the best, His Holy Spirit.

When you are bound by sickness or tempted by lust and other sins there is a way out by using the name of Jesus Christ.

We see an example of the power we can have in His name when Peter said in Acts 3:16, *"Jesus' name has healed this men-and you know how lame he was before. Faith in Jesus' name-faith given us from God-has caused this perfect healing"* and in Acts 9:34 *"Peter said to him. "Aeneas! Jesus Christ has healed you! Get up and make your bed." L.B.* And he was healed instantly.

Here we see Peter healing this man by the authority of Jesus Christ. When the paralyzing spirits was cast out he was able to <u>walk</u>. He was set free from the bondage that Satan had kept him in. These are the sign that will follow the spirit filled believer who use the power of Jesus' name in Marc 16:17-18

Most preachers teach that you have to fight to control your flesh and bring it under discipline. They will tell their flocks that when they transgress to bring it to the cross, confess their sin, and everything will be erased. This is true but it is not the whole picture. Many do not tell their people that the battle is a spiritual one. As a result, people are kept in a slumbering state always walking in defeat, bent backed and having no victory.

The Bible tells us in Eph. 6:12, ***"For we wrestle not against flesh and blood, but against principalities, against powers, against the rulers of darkness of this world, against spiritual wickedness in high places."***

As explained in the verse above, it was to destroy the works of the devil that our heavenly Father gave the gift of discerning of spirits (1 Cor. 12:8-11) to recognize what oppresses or controls the souls of men. You are going to wrestle against principalities, dominions, powers of darkness, and evil spirits in the spirit realm.

However, through the gift of discernment, the Holy Spirit reveals the entrapments, the schemes, and the plans that Satan is using to enslave the souls of mankind in the name of Jesus.

Our weapon against Satan is our knowledge of the scriptures and since we are fighting a spiritual war we have to use spiritual weapons. We see in 2 Cor. 10:4, ***"For the weapons of our warfare are not carnal, but*** *mighty through God to the pulling down of strongholds."* **KJV**

God has given us the ability and authority to say "no" to Satan when we belong to God. We are instructed in James 4:7, *"**Submit yourselves therefore to God. Resist the devil** (not the flesh) **and he will flee from you.**"* KJV

The Christian person has to be vigilant and always on guard for he is in contact day by day with unbelievers. He needs on a daily basis worldly things for his substance. The enemy will try to put pressure and harass you with temptation by your worldly contact. Good behavior are strengthened by exercise and discipline.

Our Lord promised to protect those who have faith, are humble before God and resist in prayer. God's blessings come to those who are doers of the word. Jesus came to break the chains, and to set the captives free (John 8:32). They will be protected from the power of darkness according to Psalms 91, *"**We live within the shadow of the Almighty, sheltered by the God who is above all gods. This I declare, that he alone is my refuge, my place of safety; he is God, and I am trusting him. For he rescues you from every trap, and protects you from the fatal plague. He will shield you with his wings! They will shelter you. His faithful promises are your armor. Now you don't need to be afraid of the dark any more, nor fear the dangers of the day; nor dread the plagues of darkness, nor disasters in the morning.* Though a thousand fall at my side, though and ten thousand are dying around me, the evil will not touch me. I will see how the wicked are punished but I will not share it. For Jehovah is my refuge! I choose**"* *the God above all gods to shelter me. How then can evil overtake me or any plague come near? For he orders his angels to protect you wherever you go. They will steady you with their hands to keep you from stumbling against the rocks on the trail. You can safely meet a lion or step on poisonous snakes, yes, even trample them beneath your feet! For the Lord says, "Because he loves me, I will rescue him; I will make him great because he trusts in my name. When he calls on me I will answer; I will be with him in trouble, and rescue him and honor him. I will satisfy him with a full life** *and give him my salvation." LB* We stand on these promises in the name of Jesus Christ.

Chapter 16

Forgiveness

To be healed of every injustice done to you by others, one has to learn to forgive. Jesus forgave us our sins and now He wants us to do the same for others.

Some people blame God for the miserable life they live, not realizing that they are blaming the wrong person. The perpetrator of this unhappiness is the counterfeit (Satan) and he is having a good laugh at your expense.

A person will say to me, "I have a confession to make. I hate my husband. I even pray for God to come and take my husband. I don't care how God take him; just get him out of my sight."

The enemy, the devil is the perpetrator of these marriage troubles and yet spouses are asking God to release them from their vows. Can you imagine! They have been miserable for so long that they want out of it. They are even pleading for God to commit murder so they will be free. I am appalled at Christian people talking this way.

If you choose to walk in the sandals of Christ, then forgiveness must be present in your lives. You can't pray, "Lord Jesus, I love you and I want to live for you but I cannot forgive my mother for the way she treated me; I cannot forgive my ex-husband for jilting me for another woman; I will never forgive my father and brothers for abusing me sexually." And the list goes on and on.

The reason so many believers cannot receive healing or deliverance is because they are being deceived by the work of the counterfeiter, our worst enemy. Forgiving the hurts, bruises, pains and wounds that were inflicted on you through the years is necessary if you want deliverance.

In Matt. 5:22-24 we see, *"But I have added to that rule, and tell you that if you are only angry, even in your own home, you are in danger of judgment! If you call your friend an idiot, you are in danger of being brought before the court. And if you curse him, you are in danger of the fires of hell. So if you are standing before the altar in the Temple, offering a sacrifice to God, and suddenly remember that a friend has something against you leave your sacrifice there beside the altar and go and apologize and be reconciled to him, and then come and offer your sacrifice to God."* LB

Here are steps to receive God's forgiveness: First, you must repent and be sorry for sins you have committed, followed by a determination to turn away from sin or have a firm resolution not to do it anymore.

Second, you must renounce, which means to give up, abandon habits or make a clean break from the works of darkness.

Third, you must be willing to forgive and pardon all the guilty ones who have done you wrong in any way and release all the resentment, bitterness, anger, hate and rage against those who have injured, wounded and damaged you in any way.

Fourth, release the spirit of offense that you carry against the guilty one who has criticized and belittled you, etc. These are the steps to receive His forgiveness.

Matt. 6:12,15 states, *"And forgive us our sins, just as we have forgiven those who have sinned against us. Your heavenly Father will forgive you if you forgive those who sin against you; but if you refuse to forgive them, he will not forgive you."* **LB**

You must forgive or your heavenly Father will not forgive you and you will hinder your spiritual growth. Forgiveness doesn't mean to let others abuse you or take advantage of you. This is not what forgiveness is all about. Here is an example of what I mean:

A woman had a husband who was so lazy he was not working to provide for his household. He abdicated his role as head of his family, neglecting to supply the needs of his wife and offspring.

His spouse was working ten hours a day to provide for food, rent and needs of their children and her husband. She was being manipulated and controlled by him who was brainwashing her to take this abuse. She was getting more resentful and bitter towards this lazy bum who was living like a king at her expense.

When she confessed her resentment and unforgiveness to her pastor he told her that she was to forgive. He was right. She was to forgive, but she was not under any obligation to endure this kind of treatment.

As a Christian, it was her duty to set boundaries and show her lazy husband that if he wanted to eat he was to work. This environment was destroying her. He was lazy and sluggish and didn't want to take his responsibility and neglecting the need of his family.

She gave him an ultimatum. She packed his suitcase and told him to provide and take his rightful place as the head of the family or get out. He chose to work. She was set free of her anger and she regained her peace.

You do not let others abuse or misuse you under any condition or circumstance or deception. You do not become a doormat to every kind of exploitation. By forgiving it releases you of the burden, stress and oppression you are under.

First, it's between you and God. Second, it's between you and the other party you are holding a grudge against. Third, by forgiving and showing the other person where they are wrong then the healing process can begin.

It is not by continuing to be a martyr, trying to take all the responsibility on your shoulders but by putting a stop to it. This is what forgiveness is all about.

I will give you another example of forgiveness.

A woman who was abused by her father and brothers came to see me for deliverance. During the session, the Holy Spirit began to reveal the spirits of sexual abuse. Memories of those defiling moments flooded her and she was overcome with uncontrollable sobbing. The emotions of shame, humiliation and guilt overwhelmed her. Each minute detail was as vivid in her mind as though it had happened yesterday.

I cradled her in my arms like a small child and asked the Holy Spirit to bring healing to her. From her wounded heart she cried, "I can't forgive! I have no self-worth, and I have an intense fear of men. Every time my husband approached me for intimacy I froze in terror. My life has been one abuse after another."

I said, "Sweetheart, are you willing to ask Jesus to help you to forgive?"

She replied, "I don't know how."

I related to her a program I heard on the radio one day. The news was reporting the story of two young children who were being taken away from their mother because family members and neighbors had sexually abused them. On hearing this, I had become filled with anger and prayed, "Please Lord, punish those people for what they have done."

The Holy Spirit answered me gently saying, "Who was praying for those people when they were being sexually abused?"

My heart broke! I realized that Jesus wanted me to pray for the abusers as well as the abused children.

Once she realized that her abusers might have been violated the same way she was, then she was able to forgive them and was gloriously set free. There are many still suffering because they were terrorized and sworn to silence by their molesters. But their deep wounds can be healed if they are willing to forgive.

There are other people who have never been abused sexually but carry emotional bondage which are just as damaging.

If a person has been ridiculed, rejected, laughed at, criticized by remarks like "you will never amount to anything" and so on, these experiences will cause emotional damage. These negative remarks can bring hurt feelings that slowly grow into resentment and anger. Because of unforgiveness countless people are stopped from growing spiritually.

Others will ridicule or chastise someone with verbal abuse. Many lose their self-esteem and carry grudges. They live in emotional turmoil and torment because of those nasty and critical remarks that were spoken in anger. It caused tremendous hurt feeling and pain.

It is small offenses that happens everyday, which keep many in bondage. It takes only one second to open a wound and it takes years to heal it. As for others it will take a lifetime.

You have to be vigilant in the work place for worldly people will use jesting or coerce jokes to make people laugh. Those filthy languages will contaminate your thoughts and you will have a hard time to regain your pure values.

Satan is a deceiver and will throw small baits to distract you and make you stumble. It is not always big temptations that will make you fall. Sometimes these are overpowering situations and you will be guilty or start to put yourself down because of entertaining those thoughts.

Put a stop to it right away. Correct the situation by mending the problem. Rebuke and renounce those thieves of corrupt imagination and their supporting network of spirits, in the name of Jesus. If you have hurt someone, go and ask forgiveness. Clear the air and make amends. It will bring peace and restoration.

Another woman had an aversion, resentment and unforgiveness toward men after being physically and sexually abused by males in her family. She refused to forgive them. As a result, she became fertile ground for Satan to bring a cycle of destruction in her life. She lived daily in resentment and unforgiveness toward her abusers.

She later became a Christian but continued to be tormented by recurring ungodly thoughts. Although she was plagued with insomnia, stress and depression, she didn't reveal her secret to anyone. By keeping these abuses secret she became an accomplice and a cooperator with the abuser.

I asked her, "How do you relate to men in your workplace?" She admitted that she hated them with a passion and resented them but had never understood why. She said, "I have a difficult time relating to men because I'm so afraid of them." She was able to relate to women without fear because she didn't feel threatened by them.

The spirits of unforgiveness, lesbianism, fear of men, fear of being attacked, abhorrence to sex, childish self-will, frigidity, and hatred for men were discerned. When these spirits where exposed to the light, she was able to forgive the men who abused her. She was set free of these spirits and was also able to let go of the blame she placed on herself for the abuses.

It has been months now and she is regaining her self-esteem and confidence. Praise the Lord for the victory in her life.

Although my examples have consisted mainly of women, I have also seen the same kind of sexual abuse with some of the men who have come to be set free. Many were threatened and forced to cooperate with the abusers.

When children are sexually abused, their bodies and thoughts are prematurely exposed to sexual pleasures. They may begin to search for occasions to abuse others and may also become attracted to others who are bound by the same kind of lust.

Fear in children often keeps the abusers safe from discovery. Even when some children have dared to verbalize and denounce their abusers, they were often called liars.

Later in life when abused men marry, they will often use their wives as sexual objects instead of soul mates. These men have testified that they have no respect for women in general; they criticize, belittle, and treat them as objects. Because they have been violated, they want to hurt others the same way that they've been hurt. They feel unclean, and they have no self-respect.

When the spirits of hate for women, lust, homosexuality, fear of homosexuality, perversion, accomplice, cooperation, adultery and fornication were revealed in these men, they were able to forgive their abusers. They were delivered and set free of these controlling spirits and the love for women was restored.

Chapter 17

Walking in Victory

Our Heavenly Father wants to bless us daily. His desire is for us to grow spiritually. This happens when we choose to be obedient and loyal to Him. He never created us to be like robots only to follow predetermined commands.

God has created us to be free to choose between what is good and what is evil. With freedom comes responsibility. It is our responsibility to guard our minds as Satan is always tempting us to disobey God. We are not fighting against flesh and blood but against the powers of darkness as explained in Eph. 6:12, *"For we wrestle not against flesh and blood, but against principalities, against powers, against the rulers of the darkness of this world, against spiritual wickedness in high places." KJV*

The ministry of deliverance was not practiced or explained for many generations and few knew how to cast out evil spirits. God's people endured all the bondages of Satan because they lacked the keys to break his power. Hosea 4:6 says, *"My people are destroyed for lack of knowledge: because thou hast rejected knowledge, I will also reject thee, that thou shalt be no priest to me: seeing thou hast forgotten the law of thy God, I will also forget thy children." KJV*

When you were in darkness and living in sin you were groaning in pain and mental torment. But now you can have victory from the bondage that the enemy has kept you under for so many years. You are always a target of the enemy who will try to tempt and influence you. Developing strength takes time. You must be ever vigilant.

Unfortunately, we live in an instant society. The need for instant gratification spills over into our spiritual lives. Many, after being set free from the spiritual bondage of particular spirits, want instant victory over the habits and behavior patterns formed as a result of allowing these evil spirits to operate. Instead of praying and waiting on God to show them how to walk victoriously, many run to a person who has the gift of discerning of spirits for deliverance.

We must learn to resist the devil through prayer. Obedience to God is often learned by the daily trials we go through. Our character is strengthened as we learn to trust God more through each struggle and to lean on Him. He gives us victory over the enemy.

Trials are often for our own good as seen in Rom. 5:15. Here are some steps to walking in victory:

Every morning ask God to place a hedge of protection over, under and around you, your husband, your wife, your children, your house, your workplace, your family, your school, etc. with the precious blood of Jesus.

Take the time to pray for the government and the leaders.

Resist every attack the enemy hurls at you. Don't be fooled when the enemy tries to convince you of his power. He has none if you don't give him any. The deceiver lost his power when Jesus gave his life on the cross to set us free.

In Jesus we are more than conquerors through Him that loved us according to Rom. 8:37-39). Take your authority in the name of Jesus and resist him. James 4:7 tells us to, *"Resist the devil and he will flee from you."* *KJV*

When you as a Christian pray this prayer, it is important to be sincere in order to overcome whatever problem is hindering you. When you put up a spiritual battle to recapture the ground that satan has stolen from you, be sincere. Matt. 12: 43-45 tells us there is penalty for those who say they are sincere when they are not genuine.

It is important to study the word. Keep in prayer and invite the Holy Spirit to be in charge.

If you are praying for yourself and asking the Holy Spirit to reveal areas of bondage, a word such as fear or hate, etc. may come to your mind. This is the oppressing spirit revealing itself. Rebuke these spirits by praying the following prayer:

Prayer of Self-Deliverance

"Father in the name of our Lord Jesus, I break, renounce and bind the spirit of--- ---(replace by other revealed names of spirits) that is in me going back through the womb up to ten generations on both sides of my family. I break every curse. I destroy every legal hold and ground that satan has against me. I break every inherited spirit from my forefathers that is in me right now in Jesus' Name."

Repeat this prayer every time the Holy Spirit reveals the name of oppressing spirits. You'll notice that many of the spirits came through the womb from your forefathers. If you don't break the curse now they will be passed on down to your children.

If your children were witnesses to your reckless and permissive conduct before you became a Christian, they may have become fertile ground for Satan to continue the same destructive ancestral behavior.

You may not be aware of the sins of your forefathers so break every curse that has come through the family line up to ten generations (Deut. 23:2).

If you are seeking deeper healing or are having trouble identifying all the names associated with a certain spirit it helps to look in a thesaurus to get a broader scope of names which may be attached to the original spirit.

Of course you won't have all the names that are shown in the thesaurus but the Lord will reveal which ones you are bound with. Then pray the prayer of self-deliverance.

The biggest battle that is being fought today is the battle for the mind. Satan knows that his time is short and he's using various methods in his quest for control of our minds. By bombarding the mind through T.V., books, magazines, videos, movies, music, etc., he desensitizes and confuses our moral codes, making good seem bad and bad seem good and weakening our sense of right and wrong.

So be careful what you allow to enter your mind, what you watch on T.V. or the materials you read or the kind of friends you associate with.

Be careful of the words you speak. Often times, words spoken only once become a curse in someone's life and their loved ones. Sin can easily come into the mind when it is not protected. Satan cannot come in without your permission.

You are the gatekeeper. The enemy wants man to be a slave to sin. He will use any method to force his way in since that is the only way he can propagate confusion in the heart of man. He needs someone or something to promote his filth. He will use memories that you long to forget and habits from which you would long to be free.

Other areas that he will use is pornography, mental abuse, lust, incest, bondage to fears, habits you want to get rid of, alcoholism, mental torment, rebellion, occult practices, false worship, etc. Satan knows that when you have freedom he loses his channel for doing his dirty work. His power is broken when you are set free.

In Rom. 6:14 we see that, *"For sin shall not have dominion over you: for ye are not under the law, but under grace." KJV*

As you grow in your relationship with the Lord and become more attuned to the voice of His Spirit, you may sense Him leading you to help others become free from the bondage of the destroyer. With a prayer partner constantly holding you before the Lord, pray the following prayer and cast him out.

Prayer of Deliverance

"Father in the name of our Lord Jesus Christ, I come boldly before your throne to ask for guidance and wisdom in this deliverance. Lord, in Jesus' name, I ask that you intervene in this person's life. I ask that you break every control that Satan has over his/her life. Break it right now, in Jesus' Name. I renounce and break every principality, every dominion, every power of darkness, and every evil spirit in the spiritual realm. I bind and break every assignment that they have over (the person's name) right now in Jesus' name. And now Lord, I ask for your protection over, around and under my house and over every member of my family (I do the same thing for my praying partner and their household). I ask Your Holy Spirit to guide me and to give me wisdom. I cover each one of us in this room with the precious blood of our Lord Jesus, so that no transference of spirits can take place, in Jesus' Name. Now I command every spirit that is controlling (the person's name) to name themselves right now in Jesus' name. (I often pray in tongues at this point and wait for the Holy Spirit to name the spirits by interpretation.) In the name of Jesus I command the spirit (by name) to come out."

The person may cough, sneeze, yawn or sigh. Tears may roll down their cheeks or there may be no demonstration at all. Everyone who has faith in the name of Jesus can do deliverance because His name is powerful enough to cast out spirits and bring freedom.

But first make sure that you have been set free from your own bondages. Go through the deliverance process yourself before you try to deliver others.

God will respect each person and will not force His will on you. He wants you to be free. Jesus paid a dreadful price for us so that we could be set free of Satan's dominion.

The biggest battle that is fought right now is the battle of the mind. But remember we have hope in Jesus Christ. On Calvary He disarmed Satan, made a public spectacle of Him and triumphed over him (Col. 2:15). Jesus shed His precious blood to cover the sin of the world.

You can have victory and conquer the bondage that keeps you a prisoner in the flesh. You can choose who your master will be. God wants you to be free. But the choice is yours. You must invite Jesus to be your Lord and Savior. He cannot do it unless you invite Him in. He will not force His will on you.

The choice is yours to make. Joshua made his and challenged his people in Joshua 24:15 when he said, *"Choose this day whom you will serve."* Who will you serve? If you choose God's way then Jesus said in John 8:32, *"And ye shall know the truth, and the truth shall make you free." KJV*

Books Available

Discerning of Spirits the Unknown Gift
Deliverance for Yourself and Others

Written in English and in French
To order Additional copies write to:

Odette Ouellette
P.O. Box 24
Russell, Ontario
K4R 1C1

U.S. Orders: $12.00 U.S. plus $2.50 shipping per book
Canadian Orders: $15:00 Can. plus $1.50 shipping per
book

Book(s) $----------------

Sales Tax $----------------

Total $ -------------

Shipping and handling $--------------

Grand Total $---------------

N.B. No C.O.D. or phone orders

Send Canadian Money Orders